SOUTH AMERICA: RIVER TRIPS

Volume II

Tanis & Martin Jordan
All Maps, Drawings & Photos by Martin Jordan

Published By:

Bradt Enterprises Inc.
95 Harvey Street
Cambridge, MA — U.S.A. 02140

To the memory of
Claude Blamey,
Hannah Jordan, and
George Jordan

Copyright©1982
Tanis & Martin Jordan

Reproduction of this book, in any manner, in any language, in whole or in part, is prohibited by the International Copyright Agreement. Under it all rights are reserved by the publisher.

The authors have done their best to insure all information appearing in this book is totally accurate. However, they can not be held responsible by readers who are in any way inconvenienced or delayed.

The quotation from RIVERS OF THE SINGING FISH has been reprinted with permission of the publisher, Hodder & Stoughton.

Library of Congress Cataloging in Publication Data (Revised)
Main entry under title:

South America: river trips.

   Vol. 2 by Tanis and Martin Jordan.
   Includes bibliographies and index.
   1. South America — Description and travel — 1951- — Guide-books. 2. Rivers — South America — Guide-books. 3. Boats and boating — South America — Guide-books. 4. Natural history — South America. I. Bradt, George. II. Bangs, Richard, 1950-
F2211.S67   918′.0438   80-69523
ISBN 0-933982-13-5 (v. 1)   AACR2

Amid the treacherous marshes and baleful vegetation a marvellous crimson flower grows on the banks of the Ucayali. The natives call it the situli. It has two rows of heart-shaped calyces, each as large as a human palm and of a scarlet so brilliant and vital that they seem to burn in the twilight of the jungle. You stand dazzled, lost in ecstasy at the sight of it. And you feel that it was worth while journeying to the ends of the earth just to see the situli *flower.*

ACKNOWLEDGMENTS

We wish to thank those people who, over the years, have helped us in our traveling career (and we hope will continue to do so!).

Thanks must go first to that maker of tents, hammocks, clothes, and kit bags, writer of letters and sayer of prayers, Tanis's mum, Emily Blamey. And thanks to our untiring modifier of inflatable boats, designer of equipment, and giver of good advice, Graham Blamey (Tanis's brother; we keep it in the family – it's cheaper!), nobly supported by Ginny and Gabby.

Thanks also to all of you who have assisted and supported us in so many various ways: Gladys Buck, Patsie Proctor, Dominic Jordan, Dr. W. Brace, Jaime and Hazel Garcia – ¡muchas gracias!, Prof. J.L. Cloudsley-Thompson, Rosemary Lowe-McConnell, Dr. Ramon Ferreyra, Dr. Al Gentry, Dr. J. P. Schulz, Brad Booker, Claudette and family, Pam Fiorentino, Paul Gammons (wherever you are), Julia and Bob Morley, Rudy and Gerti Truffino, John and Lil Forbes, Kath Hetherington, Angela Roland, the late Sisto Castillo, Mrs. Keys, Mark Mardon, Ivan Augsburger, Prof. C.G.G.J. Van Steenis, Horty and Johnny de Bruin, Rainier Kame, the late Bishop and Mrs. Marshal, Brian and Bobbie McGann, and Jean May.

Finally, thank you to the British Naturalist Society, The Open University, Arnold's Travel Service, Batchelor Foods Ltd., Paul Hancock Photographic Ltd., Avon Rubber Co. Ltd., and Worby's Pharmaceutical.

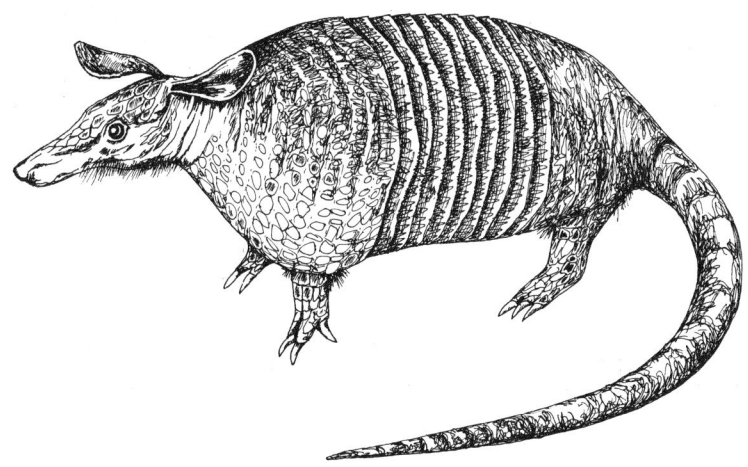

Nine-Banded Armadillo
Armadillos range in lenth from the fairy armadillo at a mere 12 cm. to the giant armadillo at 1½-m. Armadillos give birth to two pairs of identical twins at each birth.

INTRODUCTION

In the first volume of this South American river trip series, George Bradt introduced the idea of using river travel as a rewarding means by which to see a country, rather than merely as a slow way to get from one place to another. Boat journeys were represented as an exciting and challenging alternative to backpacking and riding in motor vehicles, with accounts of experiences ranging from a safe and comfortable voyage by passenger steamer down the majestic Amazon all the way through to a hair-raising, white-water raft expedition down a fierce, dangerous mountain river.

Continuing the theme with this second volume in the series, my wife Tanis and myself offer a more specialized selection of river journeys that we've undertaken in recent years. Our own idea of a good expedition is to get out onto a jungle river in a small boat, without the company of native guides or boatmen, and to stay away from civilization for several months. This preference of ours for wilderness and aloneness leads to comments such as "I would love to do the kind of traveling you do, but how do you go about it?" (and others who say, "I wouldn't make a trip like one of yours for a million dollar!").

With the former in mind, we've provided a lot of intensely practical information of the "where, when, why, and how" variety that we believe will be useful not only to potential expeditionary travelers but to anybody contemplating any kind of journey in tropical South America.

Finally, by adding a few words about ourselves, I shall attempt to convince you that adventure travel is a possibility open to anyone who is sufficiently motivated. In terms relative to the affluent society in which we both live, Tanis and I are neither wealthy nor privileged. We save the necessary traveling money from doing ordinary, mundane work, yet without too much difficulty or sacrifice manage regularly to take ourselves to areas few people visit and occasionally to places where nobody has been before us. Nor did we begin our exploring career with any speical qualifications. So if in this book we describe the kind of trip you have always dreamed of making, yet never considered a serious possibility, it is quite likely that there is really nothing stopping you from doing something similar yourself.

....

We are the editors of this series, so if you have taken any interesting river trips (or if you take any after reading this book), we would like to hear from you.

Contents

Acknowledgements 5
Introduction 6
Planning a River Expedition 9
Restrictions and Red Tape 10
Whom to Write To 10
Raising Money 11
Expedition Shopping 12
Choosing a Boat 12
Tents 14
Hammocks 14
Other Equipment 16
Jungle Clothes 16
Photography 17
Food 17
Words to the Wise 21
Traveling Companions 21
Jungle Etiquette 22
Medical Precautions 22
Fitness for An Expedition 23
Keeping the Parasites Out 24
Small Menaces 24
Snakes 25
Finding Your Way 30
Don't Get Lost 30
Camping 32
Fire 33
Rapids and Other River Hazards 33
The Jungle World 37
The River System 37
Water Types 39
Oxbow Lakes 39
A Remarkable River Plant 40
Fish 40
Indian Fishing Methods 43
Jungle Ecology 44
In the Jungle 46
Jungle Sounds 50
Creek Drifting 50
River Gold 50
Venezuela 53
Canaima National Park 53
Carrao River and Aonda Canyon 54
Churun Canyon and Angel Falls 58
Surinam 63
Wildlife Conservation 63
Coastal Nature Reserves 64
Forest Nature Reserves 64
Brownsberg Nature Park 65
Raleigh Falls/Voltzberg Reserve 66
Bigisanti Beach, Wia Wia Bank 70
The Tapanahoni River 78
The Wayana Indians of Southeast Surinam 87
Canoeing in Brazilian Amazonia 93
Peru 103
Manu National Park 103
About the Authors 110
Bibliography 111
Index 115

MOT – MOT, ORCHIDS & LEAF INSECT

Planning a River Expedition

For us, five or six months is a suitable period to spend traveling. Any longer and we find that we become saturated and cease to appreciate the new things we see and experience. The places we visit are invariably sparsely populated jungles and we travel by small boat on the rivers. This is the kind of trip we enjoy most.

Our initial inspiration for a trip might come from a book, magazine article, TV program, or whatever. Having decided where we want to go and what we want to do there (be it search for Inca cities or have a look at a tropical rain forest), we calculate the trip's approximate cost. At this point we usually have to put the hoped-for departure date back by one year.

The next stage is letter-writing. We write to every possible source for advice and information and this can mean writing hundreds of letters. If we plan to go into a national park or an area to which access might be regulated in some way, we apply for permission at least six months and preferably one year in advance of our intended visit. If all this seems like a lot of hassle, it's worth remembering that the most interesting places cannot be visited by casual travelers acting on a whim. If your first letters aren't answered, write again — and again. If you're planning something unusual, chances are that it hasn't been done before in that country and officials aren't sure how to handle you; be persistent. You will have to convince them that you are serious, competent, well prepared, and possibly experienced at what you want to do. Include letters from organizations recommending you (an impressive letterhead goes a long way) and a plan of where you want to go and what you want to do. However, don't be put off if they say at first that something is impossible; there's a first time for everything. (A lot of townsfolk, including ministers of the interior, have a deep suspicion and fear of the jungle and will do their best to put you off.) But do be prepared to be flexible in your plans since you don't know the country.

Restrictions and Red Tape

The reasons that the authorities in many South American countries endeavor to keep people out of certain jungle regions are many and varied and, contrary to popular belief, it's not always because there are things going on that they don't want the outside world to know about. For instance, if a party of adventurers fails to return to civilization when they are expected, a costly search might have to be mounted. Although the age of the hunter/gatherer people is drawing to a close, there are still places left where uncontacted or aggressive tribes of people live. Here irresponsible travelers can create unfavorable impressions among the people toward the outside world. Primitive people can accidently be infected by modern man's diseases with fatal results. Travelers might even get themselves massacred, which isn't simply a case of "hard luck for them, but they knew the risks they were taking." It's also very bad PR for the Indians. Also, even when a wilderness is protected from timber exploitation, road building, or similarly destructive large-scale projects, casual access to all and sundry necessarily means an influx of gold and gem prospectors, skin hunters, misguided religious zealots, and others capable of destroying the forests, decimating the wildlife, and eliminating ancient cultures in a remarkably short period of time.

So when you plan to go off into the wilds, there's no need to automatically imagine sinister happenings simply because you find yourself having a hard time obtaining an official permit from the ministry. If you're patient, persistent, and polite, you'll probably get the access you want.

Whom to Write To

These agencies can provide much valuable information.

Embassies. Write to your country's embassy in the country of your destination. You can also write to other embassies, but remember, keep your letters as brief and to the point as possible.

Ministries. You can get a lot of essential advice from ministries, but compose your letters carefully. Again, be brief in your first inquiry, use good paper, type your letter, and be clear and precise. Don't expect ministries to answer trivial questions. Finally, it is most important to thank each ministry for their reply. Direct any further letters to the person who signed the reply (even if it's the country's president!).

Tourist Boards. These should give you any addresses you need, e.g., those of ministries and embassies. They are usually very helpful with details and sometimes have knowledge of product availability.

Airlines. Apart from information concerning transport to and within a country, airlines often answer other queries, too. If you intend to take a firearm, check any restrictions well in advance and get a letter of permission from them to carry it on board. (Passengers' firearms are usually carried in the cockpit.)

A lot of equipment can be carried as luggage; we take our inflatable boat in a canvas bag with the floorboards in a suitcase. This limits the amount of equipment we can take. You should determine whether it's cheaper to be overweight or to freight equipment ahead, but remember, freighted equipment can be held up for months at customs in South American countries and can cost a fortune to release.

Customs and Excise. This office in the country you plan to visit will tell you of any import/export regulations. Peru, for instance, at one time had a ban on importing any recording devices.

Food Manufacturers. These companies will advise you on the availability of their products in other countries and will often sell you products directly.

Whether to write in your own language or the language of the country you are visiting is a moot point; we've had success doing either but now consider it the safest and the best policy to write in English with a copy in the national tongue because, let's face it, if your recipient doesn't speak your language, it's a lot of trouble for him to get a translation and reply; your letter may end up in the trash bin.

Raising Money

By far the hardest part of any trip is raising the money. It's almost impossible to get significant financial sponsorship. Many former sponsors simply did not receive their money's worth. It's sometimes possible, however, to obtain equipment for free or at a discount. Getting free/discount items — try and put yourself in the position of the supplier and think about what he's going to get out of it. Always fulfill your obligations; that way you'll get an even better deal the second time around.

As for raising money on your return, it's possible to sell photographs and magazine articles, but you'd be doing well if you realized 10 percent of what the trip actually cost you. If you went all out to make traveling earn money for you, you might succeed, but at the expense of the freedom that made adventure travel so enjoyable in the first place. We give talks/slide shows and it's very rewarding and enjoyable, though not really a very good way of earning money. You could, perhaps, write a book for Bradt Enterprises...

Expedition Shopping

If an item is absolutely essential to your expedition, don't rely on obtaining it in the country you're visiting; bring it with you. We once scoured the whole of Lima for metal gas tanks but had to resort to plastic. We also bought what seemed to be the only 9-h.p. outboard engine in the whole of Peru! In Peru we also had difficulty finding hammocks, whereas in Surinam they were available everywhere while tents were absolutely unheard of. Don't blindly trust information, even from a good source (except this!). At one time we were told that we would be able to stock our expedition in Puerto Maldonado, a frontier town in southeast Peru. As we discovered, this town has very little for sale normally and hardly anything at all when bad weather keeps the planes or trucks from getting in! If you're using a motorized boat, the following cannot be stressed strongly enough: Gas is a prime commodity in *all* frontier towns; if you can't find out its availability before you go, then take all you need with you. (Most trucks, buses, etc. are not averse to carrying 200 liters of gas for you, but they will charge you extra.) If you don't take gas, then take containers; these too are difficult to get outside of large towns. In places where gas is in very short supply, don't let yours out of your sight; some of it will be siphoned away by people who feel their need is greater than yours. Sorry señor, it was spilt.

Choosing a Boat

Dugout canoes can be obtained, often very cheaply, just about anywhere in South America where there are both rivers and people. They are made by carving and hollowing out tree trunks and can measure up to 15 m. long. The sides are often boarded up to increase the carrying capacity. The are heavy and leaky but very strong, hold onto the water against lateral drift, are very resistant to spin, and respond well under power. As an example, a 4-m. long dugout canoe, carrying, say, two people plus 100 kg. of equipment, will move along at 9 to 10 knots in still water when propelled by a 6-h.p. outboard engine. This power won't push you up heavy rapids, though; you'll have to haul the canoe through. Alternatively, it's perfectly possible to paddle and punt dugout canoes, but if you plan a long trip against the current you'll have muscles like the "Incredible Hulk" by the time you've finished.

Fiberglass and *plastic* canoes are fragile. You should consider this point carefully if the river of your choice contains rocky rapids. Likewise, *aluminum* boats dent and fold up like tin cans when they hit rocks. The advantage of these types of craft is that they are light, fast, and responsive under power. But fiberglass, plastic, and aluminum boats are all very light so they don't hold to the water very well unless they have a deep and sharp keel, or they are heavily laden.

The *inflatable* boat is kind to its owner. It permits quite serious errors of judgment and seldom retaliates by capsizing, sinking, or breaking up into pieces as do solid boats. Instead, when driven at high speed into collision with a jagged boulder or a splintered tree trunk, your trusty inflatable will merely hiss at you in a tired but patient sort of way, deflating slowly as air escapes from the hole you've just ripped in the tube, but still tolerantly allow you plenty of time to pull into the safety of the bank. If you want to put safety first, travel by inflatable.

Inflatables are stable and resilient to knocks, damage to them is easy to repair, they can carry relatively huge amounts of weight, and they are comfortable to travel in. But flat-bottomed inflatables don't perform well under power; they are very slow and have minimal holding ability against lateral drift. They also tend to spin. Speedboat models perform much better because they are more rigid and have keels, but this makes them susceptible to damage on rapids.

If you plan to travel upstream, you must have an outboard engine as it's next to impossible to move a loaded inflatable up a fast-flowing river by paddling, rowing, or punting. Indeed, it would probably be easier to take it out of the water and carry it through the jungle!

The boat of our choice is an Avon Redseal inflatable, 3 m. long and just the right size for us and our equipment for a two- or three-month river trip. We've modified it, making it more rigid than the design intended and enabling us to use a slightly more powerful engine than the manufacturer recommends.

(NOTE: The modifications were not made on advice from the manufacturers, Avon Inflatables Limited, South Wales, England, and may well put excessive stress on the boat.)

> WARNING: Unless you've had previous experience of boats and rivers, we strongly advise you not to contemplate setting off in your own boat. A South American river is definitely not the best place to begin learning navigation and basic boat-handling skills!

Tents

An important consideration in choosing a tent is the amount of time you plan to spend in it. You may intend only to make overnight stops, but if you're ill, exhausted, or just fed up with traveling, you may have to live in your tent for days at a time and restricted space can be very claustrophobic. The ideal tent is one that allows you to sleep comfortably while leaving a fair amount of room for stowing gear. A fly sheet is a definite advantage in heavy rain and removing it during the day helps keep the interior cool; it does provide a trap for insects, though.

Here's how to do a conversion job on an igloo-shaped tent, or one with straight sides. These modifications will help you to keep cool and let you see out. We converted a tent in this way and found it great to live in — for over six months. Cut sections of the material out of the sides and door panel to form open windows. Replace these sections with strong mosquito netting and sew them in firmly. On the outside of the tent, sew panels of any tent material over the windows at the top only so that you can roll up the panels. Velcro strips or rope ties sewn at the bottom of the windows will let you fasten them. These shutters aren't as necessary if you use a fly sheet. We're wary of zip openings on tents. If the zipper breaks you've got problems, so take a couple of meters of Velcro along just in case.

A sewn-in ground sheet is essential unless you enjoy being eaten alive by insects at night. Again, you can do this yourself. Ease of erection is of paramount importance and should be simplicity itself. Some of our worst arguments were at the end of an exhausting day while holding a ridge pole in one hand and slapping mosquitoes with the other, and hopping from foot to foot to avoid biting ants, till eventually either us or the tent collapsed with frustration. If it's a large tent, make sure one person can erect it alone if necessary. A few hooks or loops inside at strategic points means you can run a rope around and sling up clothes and other items.

A tent offers many advantages. You can read, write, and play cards or other games comfortably long into the night by lamp or candlelight. You can eat away from insects. You have privacy.

SLEEPING BAGS

Nylon sleeping bags are far preferable to blankets since they're lighter, dry more quickly, and keep you warmer. They're also very easy to sell after the trip or make suitable gifts for guides or others who help you on the way. We advise against using down sleeping bags; once they're wet they're difficult to get completely dry again.

Hammocks

We have found hammocks to be by far the most comfortable form of jungle sleeping. Plain Indian-style hammocks made of woven cotton or linen are best. Choose one that is as strong and simple as possible. You can make your own hammock, but be sure that the fabric you choose is rotproof. Fancy hammocks with built-in mosquito nets and other features are often more trouble than they're worth.

If you choose to spend all your jungle nights in hammocks, then take care in your choice. Check the strength of the ropes or cords that gather the ends of the hammock; these are usually the first part to break and when your bed collapses on a wet, black jungle night, believe me, it's not much fun. Take extra cord for repairs. It's difficult to know how strong a hammock is, but examine the stitching and overstitch it yourself if necessary. Allowing a hammock to get wet weakens it, sometimes drastically. I once washed Martin's hammock in the river and the next time he used it, it started tearing.

The disadvantage with a hammock is that if biting insects are prolific you may have no choice but to go to bed when they come out (sometimes 6 P.M.!). You can read or write in a hammock, but more social activities are difficult. Also, two in one hammock puts too much strain on it. Bear this in mind when choosing your mode of sleeping.

The choice of mosquito net is as important as the type of hammock. It must be large, loose, and seal you in completely. The slightest hole and mosquitoes will be queuing up to get in. Nets are usually made of netting, but are sometimes made of very light, closely woven material that, although stronger, is heavier and hotter than netting and not suitable for very hot, humid climates. Make sure the net is large enough to be closed up underneath the hammock without touching it. Anywhere it touches you, mosquitoes (or vampire bats) can bite you; they seem to favor the end of the nose.

Take plenty of rope for the hammock and thin nylon cord for the net. Sling the hammock high and tight; it drops up to a meter with someone in it.

A SHELTER FOR A HAMMOCK

Take two large sheets of waterproof material (we suggest 3 m. by 6 m. each) and sew Velcro around each piece so that they fit together. You can then join them to form a square, an L-shape, or other shapes. Punch eyelets around the edges at about 30-cm. intervals.

To hang the shelter, tie a rope at a high point between the two trees that support your hammock and drape the shelter over it. Pull out the bottom edges and tie them to bushes, trees, etc. Tie the shelter securely or it will take off in a storm.

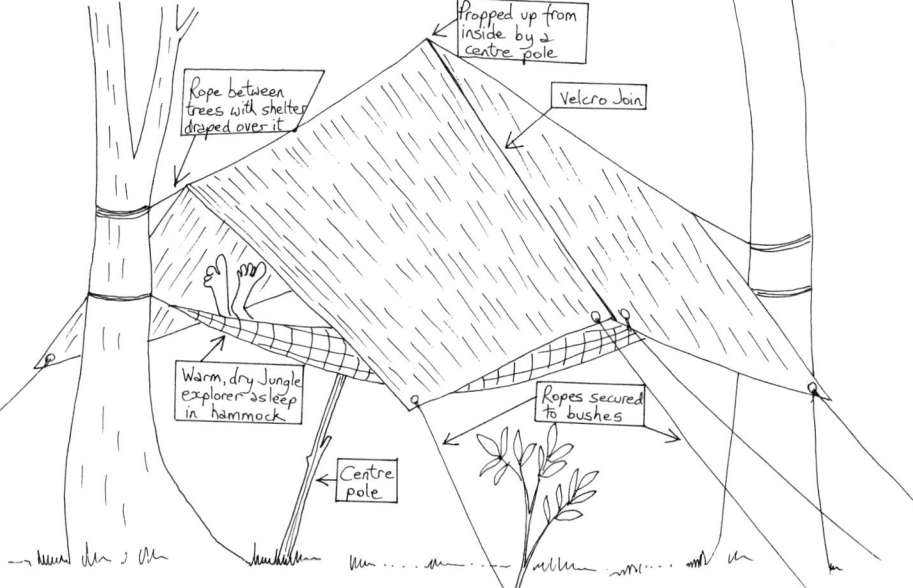

Other Equipment

Take plenty of kit bags. At first we used ex-army rubberized canvas bags, which were very tough and large. Now we make them from strong waterproof fabric with a drawstring at the neck and a couple of handles sewn to the sides. They weigh very little. A good size is 1 m. high by ½ m. across. We usually take about six bags of all the same bright color with our names written on them in waterproof marker. Traveling on public transport it's easier to keep an eye on say, bright yellow bags. We recommend keeping the bags organized by making a list of the contents of each bag. It's well worth the trouble.

Bring a coarse sharpening stone for your machete. Metal files clog up and wear smooth quickly.

Jungle Clothes

Beginning with the feet: Leather boots are not good as they become waterlogged, heavy, and rot. We wear ordinary tennis shoes. Wellington boots are occasionally useful too. Long woolen socks are comfortable and you can tuck your trousers into them; nylon socks dry more quickly, though.

We don't like baggy, voluminous trousers or shorts as they get in the way and they catch on things. Ordinary, snug-fitting trousers and shorts of some manmade, quick-drying material are recommended (stretchy materials are good). Cotton jeans are not good because they hold water too well and take too long to dry.

Underwear: Whatever you wear at home will be OK in the jungle. The way to avoid sores and rashes is to keep your body and clothes clean and (as far as possible) dry.

Long-sleeved shirts that button to the neck for protection against sun and insects are a must; you can always roll up the sleeves if you want to. Take a warm sweater for chilly nights (thick, long-sleeved sweatshirts are warm and comfortable).

A hat with a wide brim or peak will protect you from the tropical sun. On the boat, it must be attached to your head by a strap or you'll lose it within the first hour.

A voluminous waterproof cape that will go over a backpack will ward off jungle showers.

How much clothing should you take? Spares of everything will make life very much more comfortable. I wear out one pair of high-quality tennis shoes per month on an expedition. Tanis's footwear lasts much longer than this: one pair per three months.

Polyethylene is a godsend to modern explorers; the transparent stuff that's used in the building trade. You can cover or wrap your equipment with it, lay it on damp jungle floor or wet sand to sit on, shelter beneath it when it rains, improvise a 100 percent waterproof tent or cape out of it, and when you've finished with it, fold it into a tiny package that weighs next to nothing. Take plenty, say 8 m.² per person.

Photography

The opportunities for good wildlife photography on jungle river trips are less considerable than commonly supposed, even in undisturbed areas. For one thing, South American animals are notoriously reluctant to expose themselves to full view. In addition, any animals that are seen on riverbanks are invariably a long way from where you are, and in the jungle it's unusual to get an unobstructed view of anything more than a few meters away. Photographers also face the technical problems of dim light among the trees and very bright conditions on the river.

For the kind of trips we undertake, two cameras with zoom lenses are useful. One is loaded with fast film for jungle and twilight shots (early mornings and evenings are the times you will see most animals), the other with slower film for the intense light encountered on the river.

The preceding advice applies to casual photography: how to get pictures of those things you happen to see. Serious wildlife photography is an art and if you want to come home with prize-winning pictures of such things as eagles, wildcats, and monkeys, you're going to have to learn the business from a professional.

It's a good idea to have a lens that enables you to take close-ups; it's a simple matter to get spectacular shots of bizarre and colorful insects.

If you seek to sell a story on your trip, the quality of the photographs is going to be of paramount importance. Glossy magazines, including those that specialize in travel, will be far less interested in where you went and what you did than in the pictures you can show them. Unfortunately, many of the most interesting trips never appear in print because of mediocre photography.

Food

"You are what you eat," the saying goes, but in the jungle "You are what you can carry to eat" is more appropriate. If you're planning to be away from civilization, you must take all you need with you. You may well come across villages where food is grown, but remember, it is their only food and they may not want to sell it to you, so don't rely on this.

In more populated places along the rivers you'll come across trading posts. Here you can often buy foodstuffs, but at high prices (it all has to be brought in). Again though, don't rely on it. We once landed hungry at a trading post in French Guyana to find all they had for sale was Chanel No. 5 perfume and red balloons.

WHAT TO TAKE

We always take a variety of Vesta dried dinners. They come in sealed packs, each with enough to serve two persons. One such pack and rice makes our main meal, eaten in the evening. Breakfast for us is always oatmeal. It's light to carry, nutritious, and filling. In addition to these basics we take soups, stock cubes, a large variety of beans, baking powder, flour, sugar, artificial sweeteners, dried milk, soft-drink powder, cocoa, tea, coffee, spaghetti, salt, vitamin C tablets, ketchup (weighty but nice), dried fruits, matches, and candles.

We always take a few "luxury" foods, too, such as instant desserts. They may seem unnecessary, but food becomes very important on long jungle trips when a lot of time seems to be spent anticipating the evening meal. Other travelers have told us of days spent drooling over the one tin of condensed milk still unopened.

To carry dry goods easily, divide large amounts into small, well-wrapped packages. Self-sealing plastic bags are good for this.

The best utensils are enamel or aluminium with handles and lids. Take two. It's worth taking a kettle. Boiling water in a pan on an open fire is hazardous: It usually tips over when it boils and puts out the fire. You can rig up a support to hang pots over the fire. Take some wire wool (steel wool) and always clean the outside of the pans as well as the inside. It's a tiresome job, but smoke-blackened pans make everything they touch dirty and greasy when traveling. You can also use sand or gravel to clean them.

RECIPES

Here are some simple foods for campfire meals.

Stick bread. Mix flour, water, and baking powder to a smooth dough; knead thoroughly. Divide dough into sections and pull each into a long sausagelike shape. Wind each piece around the end of a green stick in a spiral. Bake over a hot (not flaming) fire for about one hour.

Oat cakes. Mix equal parts oats and flour, add sugar to taste. Add a pinch of baking powder (optional) and a pinch of salt, then mix with water to a stiff dough and shape into cakes. They can be as large as you wish to make them but the smaller they are the crisper they cook. Bake over a hot fire or fry in oil till thoroughly cooked. You can omit the sugar and eat them with savory food. Or omit the oats and just use flour — dull but filling.

White rice. Many people find it difficult to prepare white rice successfully. This method is foolproof. Wash the rice thoroughly, and place one part rice in pot with two parts water. Boil gently without stirring just till all the water has been absorbed, and remove from heat before the rice begins to stick to the bottom. Put a lid on the pot, wrap it in a towel, and let it stand for ½ hour before serving.

Brown rice. Brown rice is more nutritious than white rice. To prepare, rinse it then boil with plenty of water until tender.

Beans. Cook until tender, i.e., butter beans 2½-3 hours, lentils ½-¾ hour. Soaking overnight reduces cooking time by half, but kidney beans *must* still be boiled rapidly for at least 12 minutes. They can be highly toxic if underboiled. Add salt to beans after cooking. If added before, skins become tough. Soak beans in a plastic bag while you're traveling and they'll need less cooking time. If you really like eating beans you might consider taking a lightweight pressure cooker.

Bean sprouts. Put a handful of raw lentils or beans into a large plastic bag. Fill with warm water and leave overnight. On the next day prick holes in the bag and drain. Fill and rinse two or three times per day. The sprouts will be ready for use in three to four days to eat raw or to cook.

Fresh fish. Scrape off scales and clean. In round fish the entrails are in the belly; in flat fish in a cavity behind the head. Cut off the head and tail and remove the entrails; if you do this in the river, watch out for piranhas. Cut round fish into steaks, salt them well, and fry for about 10 minutes till brown, turning once. Flat fish are best in stew. Boil them in water with a stock cube and other seasonings for about 20 minutes. Add pasta, rice, or cooked beans.

LOCAL FOODS

Check food carefully when buying it in local markets. Watch for weevils, stones, and other extras in rice. It's worth paying a bit more for quality. Never assume that produce is safe to eat just because you see it on sale. If you feel inclined to try something new, ask how it is prepared for eating. Some fruits are poisonous when unripe, one type must not be eaten in combination with alcohol, and yet others have to be cooked or peeled in special ways.

   Here's a short identification of the kinds of food you may be able to get at jungle settlements.

Yucca. Large, long, root vegetable with dark-brown, fibrous skin. Peel it and boil or bake in fire. Tastes like a chestnut-flavored potato.

Cassava. A root vegetable eaten all over South America. The starchy tubers are peeled, grated, then squeezed and pressed to remove the juices, which contain prussic acid. Flesh is then baked into bread (bland but filling) and other food products. Some people are better at removing the poisonous juices than others and there is evidence of low-level chronic poisoning among some who use bitter cassava as a staple, taking the form of sight and hearing defects and affected motor skills. It is also made into an alcoholic beverage known as *cassiri* and other local names. Sweet cassava contains no poisons.

Sweet potato. Not related to ordinary potatoes. Can be white, pink, red, or purple with firm, sweet flesh. Tubers are globular or elongated. Bake in fire or peel and boil.

Plantain. Large green bananas that can be cooked in their skins either by boiling them or roasting them in embers. Can also be peeled and sliced, sprinkled with salt and fried in oil.

Paw Paw and papaya. Large fruits that ripen to orange-yellow skin color. Peel and discard brown-black seed. Flesh is orange-pink, sweet and juicy. Papaya is said to have healing properties if applied to wounds.

Mango. Comes in various shapes and sizes with tough skins ranging from green to yellow-orange and red. Large stone in center. Flesh is orange-yellow and juicy with a sweet and slightly spicy taste.

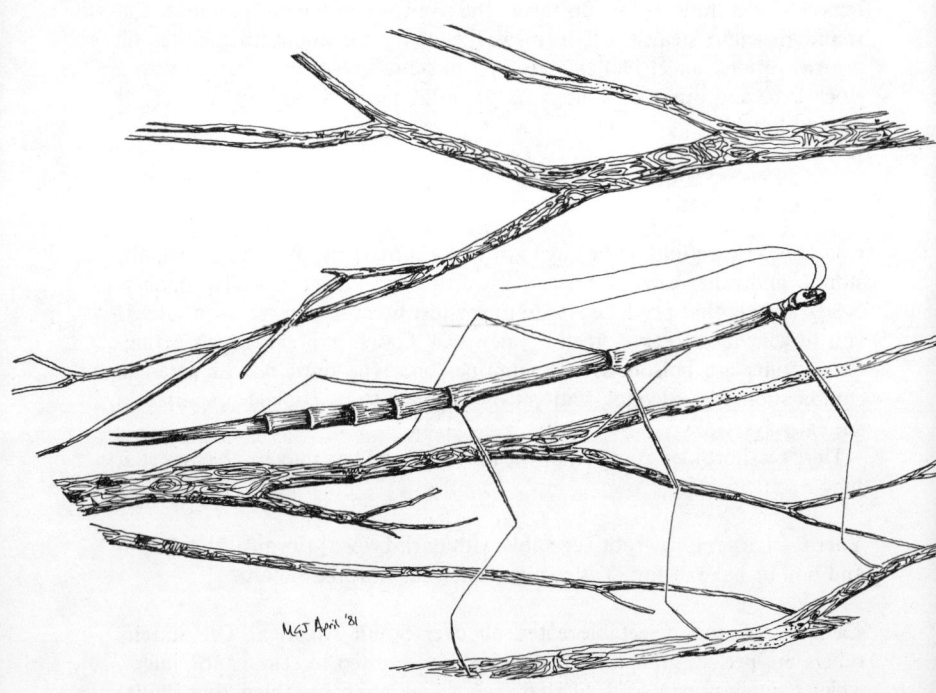

STICK INSECT

Words to the Wise

A river expedition through wild, possibly unexplored jungle can be an exhilarating experience. It can also be a nightmare. To ensure a pleasurable, rewarding trip, you should be aware of the dangers inherent in such an adventure. By heeding the pointers given in this chapter you can avoid many difficulties and be prepared for others that may arise. A South American river trip is anything but predictable.

Traveling Companions

The most common serious problem to arise on any lengthy expedition is the animosity that develops between members. Unless you've actually experienced it, it's difficult to believe the way in which mild irritation at a companion's habits can gradually develop into feelings that border on hatred. We were members of an expedition on which a normally civilized, peace-loving man attacked his friend and endeavored to throttle him because the miscreant had borrowed a toothbrush without asking! Genuinely liking the people with whom you intend to travel will go a long way toward avoiding later troubles.

A few people unexpectedly go to pieces when they find themselves leading a tough life in a strange and alien environment. They fly into rages over trivial things, sulk for days at a time, refuse to cooperate with anybody, and generally revert to childish behavior. This comes about because they are slow to make the necessary adjustments to their temporary new way of life. They'll pull out of it just so long as they are not bullied or treated with contempt; this can only make things worse for everybody concerned.

Jungle Etiquette

It's inadvisable to walk into a jungle village and begin taking photographs; in fact, it's better to let nobody see your camera initially. Some tribes hold superstitious beliefs about photographic images and become very angry indeed when somebody "steals" a picture. We once saw a man have his new Nikon camera wrenched from his grasp and hurled into the river because he took a photo of a child without asking the child's mother! Conversely, an inexpensive camera that produces instant, give-away pictures can be a useful tool for making friends.

Customarily, introductions and other formalities must be observed. In the more primitive places these are particularly important. Be attentive and respectful to the village headman and don't start casually handing out gifts of money and cigarettes. It would seem unnecessary to offer such fundamental advice but for the fact that the inexperienced often behave very strangely in novel situations; I think it must have something to do with culture shock. We saw a party of tourists in an Indian village scattering handfuls of candy over the ground for the children as if they were feeding pigeons in the park.

At some point you'll have to decide whether or not you are going to break certain health-preservation rules, such as on the occasions when you will be offered unsterilized water to drink or raw fish, rancid meat, and even dirty, much-handled food to eat. If you can't bring yourself to eat and drink what's offered, feign sickness.

If you come across a garden in the forest and you don't know to whom it belongs, leave it alone and don't touch anything. Gardens of primitive people often have religious significance and it can be regarded as a very serious offense to take fruit.

Medical Precautions

Decide early enough which inoculations you will need. Some last for ten years (yellow fever) while others only six weeks (infectious hepatitis). You may need an interval between jabs and some combine unfavorably with others. The basic inoculations are: yellow fever, cholera, tetanus, typhoid, poliomyelitis, smallpox, infectious hepatitis (gamma globulin).

You should regard countries in the tropics as malarial unless official information has been give to you that the country you're visiting is malaria-free. Point out that you intend to go into the interior . We've always taken Paludrine prophylactically. Others prefer not to take prophylactics. It has to be your own decision and the only advice we will give is to consult your own doctor or clinic. Then give the matter careful consideration; malaria can be very unpleasant.

If you plan to be out of reach of immediate medical aid, you owe it to yourself and others in your party to know how to handle serious accidents.

You should know how to inhibit bleeding, apply artificial respiration, recognize shock, and so on. Shock can follow any kind of serious accident; blood pressure drops, circulation fails, and reduced blood supply to the brain can cause death. So much good literature is available on first aid that there is little point in recommending anything here. Buy a book and study it.

WARNING: Did you know that many of the drugs that have been banned from sale in Europe and North America because of serious side effects are still on sale and widely used in third-world countries? Some of these "wonder drugs" really will clear up all manner of things, from diarrhea to stomach pains and headaches. They could also leave you deaf, blind, or paralyzed. Powerful drugs can be bought over the counter in South American countries and it's common practice to use them merely on the advice of the person behind the counter. We think this is crazy! If you're ill, get a doctor and, if you must buy medicine over the counter, make sure you can read the instructions clearly and bear in mind that it might be a drug that has been banned in your part of the world.

Keep a note of any drug you have taken while away and have a medical check-up when you get home. We've both contracted infections and parasites more than once that were only discovered at post-trip medicals! (One parasite Martin was found to be hosting would have proved very serious if not fatal if left for a few years). If you've traveled where there is resistant malaria, tell your doctor when you get back; the symptoms may not be easily recognized.

Fitness for an Expedition

It's not necessary to be any kind of athlete to undertake a tough, extended jungle river trip. To be able to run 5,000 m. in under 20 minutes or to be able to hoist a 100-kg. barbell overhead, while being no disadvantage, confers no direct advantage either. On the other hand, if you're the kind of person who suffers stomach upsets at the slightest change of diet, gets out of breath walking upstairs, strains muscles everytime you lift something heavy, and catches every germ in sight, then you'd be well advised to get youself into a better state of health before setting off on an expedition. Your age and your sex are not important, though it's our belief that women are generally a bit tougher than men in many respects, being able to get by on less sleep and less food, making less fuss about discomfort, and remaining more cheerful when the going gets rough.

Keeping the Parasites Out

In tropical countries, water can be dangerous stuff, especially the river water that flows past places where people live. The most efficient way to sterilize water is to boil it. This is not always convenient and we use water-sterilizing tablets when traveling on the rivers, doubling the dose when we think the water may be polluted. It must, however, be said that we have not always managed to keep ourselves free of infestations and some of the various roundworms, amoeba, and other animals we've hosted from time to time may well have been acquired by drinking treated water we mistakenly believed to be sterile.

The rules for tropical hygiene are so many and troublesome that you could be forgiven for thinking that it's going to be impossible to keep out parasites. We have a pamphlet that describes how, before being eaten, a lettuce leaf must be boiled for one minute then left for half an hour in a sterilizing solution! (The person who wrote it must produce some interesting-looking salads.) But one thing we've discovered is reassuring: We've never been sick in quiet jungles far away from other people. When there are people around is the time to remember not to drink unboiled water, to peel all fruit, to avoid raw, partly cooked, old, or dirty food, not to walk around barefoot, not to stroke dogs and cats, not to let beautiful, dark-eyed children poke their grubby fingers in your mouth, etc., etc., etc. Even so, in our experience you're more likely to get food poisoning after a meal in a city restaurant than after a meal in a primitive hut!

Small Menaces

Jiggers present one good reason for not walking barefoot. Beware especially of damp sandy places where the female sand fleas lurk. These tiny maggot-like creatures burrow into your flesh unnoticed and feed on your blood, becoming bloated and distended with eggs. By this time you'll have noticed painful lumps usually on your feet but also on elbows and other bare bits of you that may have rested gratefully on the cool sand. Dig out the jiggers with a sterile needle and disinfect the wounds thoroughly. I once had twenty-five on one foot alone — many under my toenails. Be warned!

Ants are incredibly abundant in the South American jungle and many kinds both bite and sting. They usually present a hazard only by virtue of their numbers; a couple dozen tiny fire ants inside your shirt is a singularly enlivening experience! There are, though, some large solitary ants whose sting is said to be quite serious. For instance, there's one in Venezuela called "ant 24" because its venom is said to produce a 24-hour fever.

We've witnessed the dreaded army ants on the march, flowing across the ground like streams of treacle ½ m. wide, the smell of formic acid wafting up from them. In daylight hours they couldn't be a real danger to anybody capable of walking, though a nocturnal visit from army ants in a jungle camp might be a serious matter.

Spiders of the furry South American kind can grow to the proverbial size of a dinner plate. They are inoffensive creatures that seldom bite and when they do it's not serious. The danger from big spiders is emotional rather than physical: We know a European man who was quite ill for a couple of days after seeing one at close quarters.

Scorpions are common enough but not frequently seen unless, like us, you enjoy turning over logs to see what's underneath (this is a potentially dangerous occupation as you might disturb a snake). Scorpions carry a venomous sting in the tail, which can, from some species, prove fatal for man. Antivenins against scorpion venom are available. Failing that, act as for snakebite and treat the pain with painkillers. None of the scorpions we've met have shown the slightest sign of aggression, though they do have a habit of crawling into unlikely places, so always tap out your footwear and shake out your clothes before you put them on. They sometimes seem amazingly lethargic. One evening I found a large scorpion and set it on a log so that I could photograph it. When I return the next day, the creature was still in the same position.

Centipedes. We've never heard of anyone being hurt by a centipede, but some of the large ones can inflict a serious, venomous "bite" from a pair of modified front legs. We once found a pathologically aggressive centipede; this 20-cm.-long animal would unhesitatingly rush forward and attack any object placed in its vicinity. (Centipede bite: as for scorpion sting, previous page.)

Tropical wasps and hornets often make nests on the underside of large leaves, artfully concealed a meter or two above the ground where people can walk into them. Some of these insects inject extremely potent venom. We have this advice straight from the lips of a Guyanese "porknocker" (gold prospector) about what to do if you accidently disturb a wasp's nest: "Drop everything, cover one eye with one hand, shut your mouth, run like hell to the nearest water and dive in!"

For a badly stung person the danger of death comes from allergic reaction, shock, and from suffocation due to swelling of the neck closing air passages. I know of no remedy but treat the pain.

NOTE: Don't sniff flowers; they may contain things that sting or bite.

Snakes

It's not unusual to spend weeks in a jungle without seeing a single snake. However, in some areas snakes are very numerous indeed. In general, snakes will be more abundant near water than away from it and more in evidence at dawn and dusk than during the hot hours of the day.

When walking in the jungle, carry a stick. Stamp your feet at intervals and the snakes will get out of your way; they don't wish to be trodden on any more than you want to tread on one.

Snakes don't chase people. No South American snake on the ground can travel faster than a human being can walk.

Constricting snakes. The boas and anacondas are the giants of the snake world. They kill their prey by coiling around it and squeezing it; they then swallow it whole. Always carry a knife so that if one swallows you whole, you can cut your way out, but don't let the snake see the knife or it may take it from you before swallowing you. (Just checking to make sure that you're concentrating.) Seriously though, there's nothing much to fear from these big snakes, but if you did accidently step on one you might receive a bad (but nonvenomous) bite. Some of these reptiles, such as the emerald tree boa, are extraordinarily beautiful creatures.

Coral snakes. These pretty snakes present little danger to humans. They are small and conspicuous with alternate bands of brightly contrasting colors. Their venom *is deadly* but they are shy, reluctant to bite, and cannot reach you through strong clothing. We once saw a small child playing with a coral snake.

Vipers. This group includes the notorious bushmaster, fer-de-lance, rattlesnake, and others. It's very, very unlikely that you will be bitten by one of these, but the remote possibility should be considered if you intend hiking and camping in the jungle.

SNAKEBITE

A few words on the "conventional" action in cases of snakebite. If you slash the puncture marks open with a blade you might cause irreparable damage to underlying tissue; you might even sever a major blood vessel and dispatch yourself or your patient. What you will certainly do is to facilitate the spread of some elements in the venom by creating easier access to the circulatory system. If you suck at the bite, you will have snake venom in your mouth; there are cases on record of people having died after assisting an injured companion in this way! (don't be a sucker). A tourniquet is of little use on its own except as a delaying measure, and if applied incorrectly can be more dangerous than the injury it's supposed to be treating. Don't give a patient alcohol unless you want to assist his demise.

This is what you should do if possible.
    1. Don't panic. *Most* snakebite victims recover, *even without treatment.*
    2. Identify, describe, or, if possible, kill the snake.
    3. Apply a tourniquet if you know how.
    4. Get the patient (and the dead snake) to the nearest medic.

If you plan to be far away from medical help, our advice is to carry antisnakebite serum that counteracts the venom of vipers, though remember that it is potentially dangerous. It is imperative that you fully understand how to use it and the inherent risks involved. The main risk of antivenin is that you may be (or may become during the course of treatment) allergic to it and you may die of shock as a result. In the U.S.A. it's manufactured by Wyeth Laboratories in Philadelphia, Pennsylvania. It is available in South

American countries, but you may have problems obtaining it. The freeze-dried varieties of antivenin are good for five years; it's an expensive but very salable commodity. We buy ours from Wyeth, carry it with us for the duration of the trip, and then sell it in South America before we return home.

Stories of Deadly Snakes

There was one topic the people of the Maracas Valley were ever eager to discuss: snakes. The surrounding green wooded hills were lovely places to walk, with huge, ancient silk-cotton trees towering above overgrown paths and deserted plantations where you could still find oranges, lemons, avocadoes, mangoes, nutmeg, coffee, cocoa, tankabean, and much else, now growing wild among the fever grass, palms, and rattling clumps of bamboo. But these places were, they told us, full of snakes, with an overabundance of mapipi *(also called bushmaster, Latin name,* Lachesis muta), *a large and particularly dangerous pit viper feared throughout the length and breadth of the continent.*

The men would only work their forest gardens between the hours of 9:00 A.M. and 2:30 P.M. because, they claimed, these are the hours when the mapipi sleeps. One day a man was cutlassing grass when he came upon a mapipi. He slashed wildly with his machete, missed the snake, and cut deeply into his own leg with the razor-sharp blade. Somehow he managed to walk and crawl to the road where he was discovered, collapsed and semiconscious. He died from loss of blood before he could be brought to hospital. A mapipi had taken a life.

We were present when a friend of our host's came to the house in which we were staying with a 25-kg. stem of green bananas across his shoulders. He'd carried them from his garden way up on the hillside and with a sigh of relief he dumped them onto the floor, then leapt backwards with a cry of alarm as a golden-colored snake came wriggling out from among the fruit. Our host, despite his seventy-six years, was a man of instant responses and with a single blow from his stick he crushed the animal's head to a pulp. This snake was an arboreal viper with a fearsome reputation for striking from low branches at the heads and shoulders of people walking beneath. Now it lay curled up on the ground, dead, but still convulsing spasmodically.

There are many widely accepted beliefs about snakes, some of them untenable. For example: Snakes can change into other animals; they will put their tails in their mouths and roll down hills like wheels; snakes take milk from goats and cows; a brood of baby snakes will retreat inside the mother when danger threatens; kill one snake and his friends will come hunting for you; cut one in half and the end with the head on it will chase you. Then there are other beliefs that are not so easy to dismiss. One of these is that mapipi will attack any light or flame. Three women were walking after sunset along a road bordered by dense brush that led to the village. The woman in front carried a flashlight to scan the ground for snakes, the one at the rear carried a flambeau (a bottle full of kerosene with a lighted rag as a wick). As they walked past a little grass-roofed shelter beside the road, the flashlight was suddenly struck from the leading woman's hand. The other two women saw clearly that a large snake on top of the shelter had done this and before they could react, it had swung around and knocked the flambeau out of the grasp of the last woman. They arrived home, shaken but unharmed, claiming that the snake had been a mapipi 3 m. long.

But in the valley (Maracas) of the snakes, quite the most public and spectacular event involving mapipi and man occurred one Sunday when two men went hunting in the hills. They carried only machetes and their intended meat was the cat-sized rodent called agouti, which they would attempt to surprise and kill with a knife blow. It happened that one of the men stepped on a large mapipi. The indignant reptile reared up and bit him on the thigh and he fell to the ground crying, "Oh God! I'm dead, I'm dead." His companion, only a short distance away, rushed to his aid where the snake promptly struck him on the back of the leg. This time its fangs never penetrated flesh but became hooked in the rubber of his Wellington boot. Feeling the impact of the strike, he jumped forward, looked back, saw the snake stretched out behind him, and began to run like crazy, believing it was chasing him. Rushing from the jungle, out onto the path down to the village he looked back again, saw the snake still there, and with energy born of blind panic he ran 3 km. at a sprinter's pace into the village.

Remember that this was a Sunday. In the village, children were playing on the street, women were washing clothes around the pumps, men were sitting on the shaded verandahs outside the stores and rum shops. Suddenly a man with a 1½-m. long snake stuck to his boot came hurtling along the main street screaming, "Save me! Save me! Save me from the mapipi!" No one stopped him — no one could catch him! But by the time he reached the far end of the village, he was closely followed by an excited, jubilant crowd of children and adults. At this point he collapsed from exhaustion. The snake was already dead, the man was given rum, and when he recovered sufficiently to tell his story, a party of villagers set forth to find his companion, who was presumed dead. But, lo and behold, the search party met this man walking down the path into the village, uninjured.

Explanation: A pit viper's retractile poison fangs are tucked away against the roof of the mouth under voluntary control and it sometimes happens that the snake will bite, without bringing them into play. That is what happened in this case, probably because the snake was just as shocked and unprepared for being trodden on as the man was to tread on it. But the tragedy was yet to come; the man who had run so far with the snake stuck to his boot was to die of heart failure later that day. The mapipi had claimed another victim.

SUBSCRIBE to EXPEDITION

Expedition is the first magazine of its kind: written, edited, printed and mailed while enroute throughout the Americas. How well it succeeds is entirely up to you. We need support through subscriptions and reader interest. Each issue of **Expedition** is filled with adventure, facts, insights, and features as diverse as latin culture, archaeology and marine life. 720-36th Avenue North
St. Petersburg, Florida
33704 U.S.A.

A Plea on Behalf of Persecuted Reptiles

Most snakes are harmless. There's no such thing as an "evil" animal yet everywhere snakes are regarded in this emotive, superstitious way and are killed indiscriminately. The effect of this on the ecology of an area is just as damaging as if birds, monkeys, fish, or any other animal were selected for extermination. Snakes are an important part of the ecosystem. If left alone no snake will bite you and all snakes will get out of your way if given a chance to do so. Please don't kill snakes simply because they are snakes. If you have a jungle guide, don't allow him to kill snakes, either.

Finding Your Way Through the Forest

The only safe method for traveling through trackless forest and ensuring that you'll be able to find your way back is by marking a path. Make cuts in tree trunks and chop down some of the low vegetation with a machete, thus creating a trail of minor destruction that you can clearly see. Blazing a trail in this way is a slow, laborious business and you'll be doing well if you cover more than 4 km. in a day. You won't see any animals because the noise will scare them away.

To gauge direction you need a compass. Sight on a tree then make your trail toward it. Once there take another compass reading and so proceed. Compasses are subject to many influences besides the earth's magnetic field. Metal ores in local rocks and even objects you carry (such as your machete) will deflect the needle, and the instrument may be particularly inaccurate in mountainous country.

It's also possible to find your way by staying within sight or sound of a river or by following a physical feature such as a ridge crest, but take care. It would be difficult to exaggerate the ease with which you can become lost if not constantly aware of the danger.

Don't Get Lost

If you were unfortunate enough to lose your boat in a very remote area, you could find yourself facing a severe test: how to stay alive. This is outside our own experience and I hope it remains so; but we have a friend who was forced to manage however he could, without provisions or tools, for nearly

CONVENTO DE LA MERCED-CUSCO (PERU)

CORINDA
GERLACH

CONVENTO DE LA MERCED
TICKET DE INGRESO

Claustro, Escaleras Monumentales, Sala Capitular y Custodia

Entrada Estudiante

Nº 8674

$ 1.00

"IPSA"—CUZCO 658—17 B

two months before finding his way to help from an Indian community. He tells of how he survived by eating ants, grubs, and snails, and by damming small streams and scooping out the tiny fish he'd trapped. He ate grass and the new shoots of innocuous-looking plants such as bamboo, ferns, and palms, though even in this he managed to poison himself on one occasion. The idea that jungles are places where bananas and papayas are everywhere for the picking could hardly be further from the truth.

If you feel the need to know more about this subject, you could probably obtain one of those jungle survival manuals that are issued to service personnel in the tropics. (You can ignore the instructions about how to make a tent from your parachute.)

You'd have to be a very unlucky traveler to find yourself stranded in this way, but it is terrifyingly easy to become lost in the jungle and this can happen as soon as you're beyond sight or sound of anything familiar.

In fact, you can be completely disoriented just 20 m. from your camp! To casually wander off among the trees and then suddenly realize that you don't know where you are is a uniquely alarming experience.

Initially, the most important thing is to resist the urge to march off in some preferred direction in a desperate attempt to retrace your steps. Wait for help. Find a tree with plank buttresses and beat them with a stick at regular intervals; the sound carries like a drumbeat through the forest and your companions will come searching for you. If you are traveling alone or if the whole party gets lost together you'll have to act, but don't do anything impulsive. Think through the situation carefully and when you do move from the point where you first realized you were lost, make a trail you can follow so you can at least return to that original spot. If you wander off aimlessly you'll walk in circles; this is not a myth, it really happens.

The need for water can become urgent and in flat country during the dry season it's not always easy to find a stream. You can look for water trapped in standing or fallen dead wood. Many types of plants depend for their existence upon catching rain water in the reservoirs at the base of the leaves. In addition to these sources several kinds of woody vines produce copious watery sap when cut, but the danger here is that if you aren't familiar with them you might select one with poisonous juices.

Question: How is it that the Indians don't get lost in the jungle?

Answer: For the same reason that observant people don't get lost on city streets: They notice landmarks and remember them.

If you travel through unmarked country with a forest person, you'll see that he constantly glances about him and repeatedly looks over his shoulder. There's a true story of an Englishman who asked his Indian guide how he had managed to lead them both back to a particular tree after hours of wandering through the jungle. The Indian explained that this was possible because the tree had not moved, it was still in the place they had left it!

Camping

It's important to remember that those delightful beaches of golden sand that look such perfect sites for pitching a tent are, in fact, a part of the riverbed. Now, camping on a riverbed, even in the middle of the dry season, is a risky business. Local people often use riverside beaches for overnight camps when traveling (it is, after all, so much more convenient than hacking out a place in the jungle), but don't get the idea that they always know best; sometimes people who have lived in an area all their lives get caught by floods and find themselves in serious trouble.

In lowland country where wide rivers meander across flat plains with few hills in the vicinity, the waters are unlikely to rise suddenly (i.e., no more than 1 m. an hour but for exceptional circumstances), and if you take certain precautions, you can greatly minimize the dangers of stopovers on beaches. Choose the highest beach you can find. Pitch your tent at the highest point beneath the forest. Pull your boat right out of the water and fix it securely. Have a rope tied from the boat to your tent; that way, if the water rises and floats the boat away, it will pull the tent down around your ears and believe me, that's about a million times better than waking up in the morning to find the boat gone! Don't leave anything on the sand when you go to bed; little things are the first to go in a flood.

The above advice applies only to lowland rivers. In hilly and mountainous country on highland rivers with rocks and rapids, it's absolutely imperative that camp be made in the forest above spate level. In this type of terrain dangerous flash flooding can occur without warning as a result of distant rainstorms. We once saw a wall of white water 2 m. high come roaring down a narrow stream bed that minutes before we could have walked across without getting our knees wet. Never, under any circumstances, camp on beaches in mountainous country.

A grove of coconut palms may look an ideal place to make camp but don't be tempted; falling coconuts are a real hazard. For the same reason, always inspect your surroundings to make sure you've not pitched your tent beneath a dead tree or one with dead boughs. Always cut down and remove any foliage where the tent will stand. Sharp roots will go straight through the ground sheet, usually just where you sleep.

Never leave the tent front open; you'll be amazed at what will fly in. To reassure the nervous, we rarely, if ever, had snakes, spiders, or scorpions crawl into our tent. Similarly, avoid leaving rucksacks or kit bags outside the tent. You'll certainly find visitors in them in the morning. Don't put your hand inside and grope around. We once left a rucksack hanging on a dead tree overnight. When I pulled a pan out of it the next morning, instantly the pan and I were covered with biting ants, which had arrived during the night. Swarms of them then ran down the tree and invaded the tent and all of our possessions.

Fire

For safety, don't light the fire too near your tent. Keep a good supply of firewood in camp and carry a supply of small pieces of dry wood in a plastic bag to your next camp.

The best way to cook on an open fire is to wait until the first fierce flames have died down and the larger wood is burning well. Don't rest pots on burning logs, though. The logs will burn through and the pots fall into the fire.

If you throw on green bushy plants, the smoke will help clear away insects.

MAKING A FIRE

Gather lots of wood, ranging in size from small sticks to small tree trunks. Pick your wood with care; green wood sometimes explodes, while waterlogged wood will never burn. Dry driftwood is excellent. If there's a fallen tree, build your fire against it.

Make a pile of dry leaves and cover it with an arrangement of small sticks. Light the kindling and gradually add wood, but don't smother the fire. Save the big pieces till last when the fire is well established. Hurricane matches are a great help for lighting fires; disposable gas lighters last only about four days.

If the kindling is reluctant to burn, add oxygen by blowing carefully into the fire and keep blowing. If the wood is damp or wet (and half the time it is), you've got problems. You can tear up a paperback or use any paper you have (ration it carefully). If as a last resort you use some gas, be extremely careful. If you soak paper or leaves, take them to the gas and don't bring the gas into the vicinity of the fire. And don't be tempted to use the gas cans as seats around the fire.

Thoroughly stamp out your fire when you finally break camp.

Rapids and Other River Hazards

If you plan to maneuver your own raft on dangerous waters, you must be proficient before your South American trip. There is no substitute for practical experience and to take on a white-water trip without the necessary expertise would be suicidal.

As a general principle, going upstream through rapids in a motorized boat is safer than going downstream. Progress is slower with correspondingly more time to make decisions and change direction. It's even possible to stop if you have to.

Some rivers contain immense quantities of timber. In the rivers of Manu Park, Peru, we've seen barriers of tree trunks 5 m. high. Timber presents a different set of boating problems than do rocks. Submerged rocks are usually indicated by surface turbulence but this is not always the case with wood, which you may not see till you're right on top of it. Whereas boulders tend to part and redirect the water, an unseen branch from a fallen tree can easily puncture an inflatable boat or overturn a canoe.

One of the most frightening things we've ever met up with was a whirlpool on the Caroni River in Venezuela. Our boat was held stationary by it for only a few moments, but during that time we could see the riverbed down the hole in the middle, like looking down a well!

It's only common sense to wear a life jacket when the going looks tricky. Having it on the seat beside you is rather like traveling in a car with the seat belt unfastened. You may feel that it's there if you need it but it won't give you any help in an emergency.

If you find yourself swept away in a rapid, turn onto your back with your legs pointing in the direction of the water flow. In this way your feet rather than your head will collide with any obstacles. Save your physical energy for steering yourself; it's impossible to swim out of the fast water on rapids.

For a description of the methods we use on rapids see Aonda Canyon and Angel Falls trip.

A River Trip Disaster

Though most of our trips have been successful, we have had our share of disasters, one of which was so severe we're lucky to be alive. We were using a fiberglass canoe and we had a few misgivings about it. It was difficult to control; it had no lateral resistance to the fast flow of the water as do dugout canoes and consequently it tended to spin, glide, and drift sideways. It was also seriously overloaded. In fact, we'd choosen a boat that was too small for our purpose, but we had either to give up the trip or go on. We went on.

The Marowijne River was very wide and we had already traversed several sets of rapids when we made camp one night just below a severe set preceded by about a kilometer of fast water. We were beginning to feel we were handling the canoe rather well by now.

The next morning we were up early, but a slight premonition made us tie our equipment to the canoe more securely than usual and we strapped on our life jackets. For the first half hour everything went well; we paddled upriver like demented turtles and made slow but steady progress. Then came a part of the river where the current was too fast for us. A glance at the bank confirmed it. We were virtually stationary. We eased our boat into the bank under the overhanging greenery and tangle of tree roots and contemplated our next move. The jungle was extremely dense, making a portage very difficult. The best solution seemed to be to keep well into the bank and to pull and paddle up through the deeper slower water. All went well and we were making progress until I (Tanis) dropped my paddle, which glided back a couple of meters and wedged itself in the bank. As we pulled further into the bank there was a sudden great splash right beside us as some large creature launched itself into the water from its hiding place among the bushes.

The front of the canoe tipped dangerously sideways and water poured in so fast that I could only shout to Martin, completely unaware in the back, "We're sinking!" Seconds later the front of the canoe sank underneath me and I was left holding a frail branch and treading the murky water. Martin was unceremoniously tipped out as the boat submerged completely. A look of utter amazement showed on his face, then he was gone, swept downstream by the fast water. I had a fleeting glimpse of all our brightly colored gear floating quickly down the rapid, then the branch broke, the current caught me, and I was dragged under. My life jacket, almost ripped off by the force of the water, popped me up to the surface and I was spun round and round until — WHAM! — a submerged tree trunk hit me in the ribs and I hung onto it like grim death. When I came to my senses I realized the predicament I was in. There was no sign of Martin and I was 5 m. out in a fast river with no way of getting to the bank.

After what seemed like hours I heard Martin calling me and to my immense relief he appeared on the bank. It was impossible to swim across that narrow stretch of surging water, so, inspired by urgency, he began trying to break down saplings to bridge the gap and rescue me. Meanwhile, I had found some of our equipment trapped against the tree underwater: the gun and a kit bag. I pulled them up and hung on tightly. Martin now had a tall sapling ready to push out for me to grab but I didn't have a free hand.

"Let go of the bags," he instructed. I wouldn't. "Let them go!" Martin yelled, by now almost dancing with rage. I let go, grabbed the branches of the sapling, and launched myself from my underwater perch as he pulled in.

We hugged one another, glad to be alive. Martin's fate had been like mine, but he had been swept much further. At one point he had been carried a meter or more under the upside-down canoe with the bags of equipment suspended by their ropes all around him as if he'd been held beneath a colorful, surrealistic octopus.

We pulled ourselves together and decided what to do. The best thing seemed to be to make our way through the jungle to a village we had seen early the day before. We had *nothing but the clothes we stood in and Martin was barefoot; at that moment we felt every centimeter of the thousands of kilometers that separated us from our home. The jungle was dense and we had to squeeze past thorn trees, clamber through lianas, and in places crawl on our stomachs. An insult to our injuries came in the person of a large red hornet that swooped down and for no apparent reason stung me on the head! Martin had grabbed a thorn tree when pulling himself out of the river and his hand was now painful and swollen (he removed the last thorn eight months later).*

After about three hours we reached the village, a cluster of dilapidated huts. Only three people were to be seen, a woman naked to the waist bent over a fire, a young boy idly poking the ground with a stick, and an elderly man dressed in a loincloth and a football jersey who sat gazing vacantly over the waters. Clearly in view was our canoe, surrounded by brightly colored kit bags still tied on. The three people obviously hadn't noticed it, or us, as when Martin called hello they turned and stared in open-mouthed wonder. We explained what had happened as best we could and though still looking a bit dazed, the man agreed to help us.

The old man took us in his canoe to retrieve what we could of our gear, which was wedged with the canoe on a sandbank. The boat was intact but badly holed, and the front seat had been ripped out. We piled everything we could find into it and returned to the village. On a large flat rock we laid out all our equipment to dry. What a mess! It was all soaked to the point of disintegration. Cameras and lenses were full of water and it poured out of the antivenin boxes. Oddly enough, the stuff in the kit bags was remarkably dry. We stayed in a hut in the village that night and by the light of a flambeau talked over the experience. We'd lost more than half our food, our cutlasses, water containers, lamps, fishing gear, clothing, letters of permission, and some money. But, tomorrow was another day and we were lucky to be alive.

After three days we were rescued by a passing canoeist and taken to Stoelmanseiland (see map). We were there for a week or two, wondering what to do next when an expedition arrived. Ten Surinamese guys in a big canoe were going on up to Indian country near the border with Brazil. We joined up with them and eventually met the Wayana Indians.

The Jungle World

For decades there has been disagreement about whether the Nile or the Amazon is the world's longest river. This dispute arises because river length is an exceedingly difficult quantity to measure. The disagreement, however, relates to river length only; in terms of amount of water carried, no river in the world comes anywhere near the Amazon.

The River System

Of the Amazon's 15,000 tributaries and subtributaries, at least 500 transport more water than the largest river in Europe and one of them, the 3,500-km.-long Madeira by itself ranks among the world's top-twenty longest rivers. It has been estimated that one third of the fresh water on earth (excluding the ice caps) is in South America and most of this is in the Amazon Basin. This basin covers some 7 million km.^{2} and is itself the largest river basin in the world.

The size of the region drained by the Amazon and Orinoco river systems can be demonstrated by superimposing a map of South America on one of North America. With the mouth of the Amazon over New York, the north bank of the river would be at Boston, Massachusetts, and the south bank at the southern tip of Long Island. The mouth of the Orinoco would then fall near the southern shore of Canada's Hudson Bay. Manaus, the city on the bank of the Amazon in the heart of the jungle, would have its counterpart on the Mexican border, flowing into the Amazon valley via Salt Lake City, Utah. The source of the rivers draining the southern Amazon valley (the Matto Grosso) would be found along the Louisiana coastline with the jungle extending southward, running off the map of North America into the Gulf of Mexico. That's a lot of tropical forest.

Lake Titicaca (an inland sea at 3500-m. elevation in the Andes) and Angel Falls in Venezuela (the highest waterfall in the world at 1 km. straight drop, twenty times higher than Niagara) are two examples of the wonders that make up the South American freshwater system. Another is the Guaira

PODOSTEMACEAE

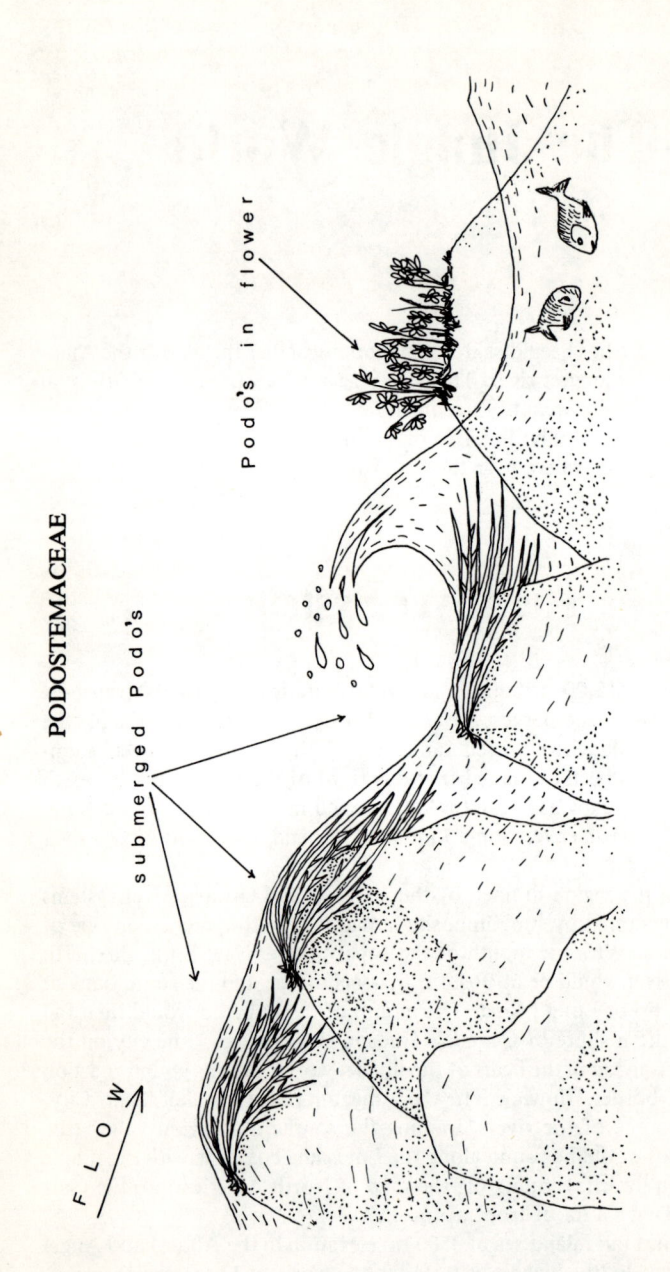

waterfall on the Upper Parana River between Brazil and Paraguay. The average flow over the lip of this waterfall is in excess of 13,000 m.³ per second, enough water to fill ten olympic-sized swimming pools every second.

South America is a land of rivers, hundreds and hundreds of kilometers of them for every single kilometer of road. If you really seek to become a part of this magnificent and mysterious continent, if only for a short while, then you must get in a boat and travel the rivers.

Water Types

South American rivers come in a variety of colors, often apparent from map names, e.g., rios Blanco, Verde, Azul, Colorado, and Negro. While many of these rivers are made murky and colored brown or ochre by suspended material, others are clear but tinted blue, green, orange, or even red by humic acids leached from dead vegetation. The red water of some rivers resembles weak tea.

The muddy, silt-laden rivers flow across low-lying country, while the transparent waters flow across country from which mud and silt had long ago been scoured. In this latter case, hard, resistant rocks dominate the landscape.

Oxbow Lakes

In the lowland forests, the rivers flow across the plains in great meandering loops and curves. As the years go by, the loops tend to migrate downstream as the water cuts away the banks, but the speed of migration varies from part to part and sometimes a loop meets part of the river downstream from it. The river then breaks through the narrow gap and a *cutoff* or *oxbow* lake is left behind. These abandoned meanders immediately begin to silt up and, like all lakes, eventually disappear.

In Peru the oxbow lakes are called *cochas* and there are scores of them along the Manu River and its tributaries, lovely quiet backwaters where birds can be seen in mind-boggling variety. In 1977 an ornithologist camped by a cocha just inside the northeast boundary of the Manu National Park. In six weeks he recorded 600 species of birds! There are not that many species of birds in the whole of Europe.

oxbow lake

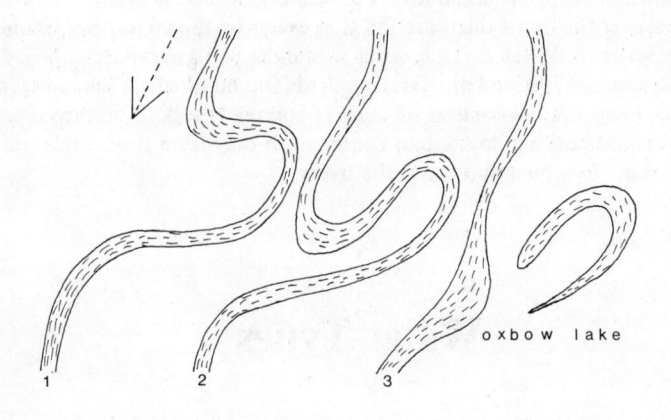

A Remarkable River Plant

Attached to the rocks of rapids and waterfalls, subjected to the fast, turbulent water, grows a plant called Podostemaceae (pronounced Poe-doe-sti-may-see; it doesn't have a common name). For much of the year these plants resemble seaweed, but in the dry season the water level falls, leaving them exposed to the sunshine. Before they shrivel and die, they dramatically burst into flower. The flowering period lasts for weeks as the water level gradually sinks, bringing more and more plants into bloom. At this time, whole stretches of wide jungle rivers become fields of purple and pink flowers, a truly magnificent sight.

Podostemaceaes are something of a botanical curiosity, exhibiting a remarkable diversity of unusual forms and structures that apparently serve no useful purposes. In some ways this conflicts with the conventional ideas about evolution, namely that genetic changes are only passed on to future generations when they confer some survival advantage to the organism involved (Darwin's theory of natural selection). On some rivers it is possible to find different species of Podos growing on almost every set of cataracts.

Fish

There are thought to be 1,800 species of fish in the rivers of South America, three times the number found in North American fresh waters and possibly as many kinds of fish as there are in the entire Atlantic Ocean.

Candiru.
What goes on beneath the surface of those inscrutable waters is no doubt just as complex and mysterious as what goes on in the treetops of the neighboring forest. Among the occupants of the waters are teeming multitudes of tiny, nameless, brilliantly hued fish, anomalous lungfish, four-eyed fish, fish that climb trees, fish that grow to over 3 m. in length, and a parasitic terror called the *candiru*, a tiny creature related to the catfish. The *candiru*, a tiny creature related to the catfish. The candiru will make its way into any available human orifice (which usually happens to be the anus or the urethra) and wedge itself there by means of needlelike spines so that surgery is required to remove it. Personally speaking, if I were a long way from the nearest hospital and forced to choose between receiving a shock from an electric eel, a bite from a piranha, a lashing from a stingray, or a candiru stuck up my ass, I'd choose any of the first three in preference to the last. The candiru provides one very good reason for never bathing naked in South American rivers.

Catfish.
In both clear and muddy rivers, numerous large, near-sighted fish scavenge the riverbed for small creatures and any decomposing flesh that happens to be lying around. Various species share this lifestyle and some of the most common, particularly in muddy streams, are *catfish*. They come in all shapes and sizes and possess long tentacles surrounding a mouth that often contains no teeth, the inside surface being as rough and abrasive as an emery board.

Because of their feeding habits, catfish are easily caught with hook and line and consequently have become an important source of high-protein food for people who live near rivers. They can grow up to 2 m. in length and their flesh can be preserved by salting and drying in the sun or in the smoke of a fire. Catfish croak and grunt and make the most peculiar noises when pulled from the water. Careless handling can result in a bad wound from the sharp spines of the fins.

Piranha.
There are many species of this common carnivore. The piranha's terrifyingly sharp teeth are capable of severing strong fishing line and I've seen one neatly bite off a chunk of wood from inside a dugout canoe when a fisherman hauled it aboard and left it thrashing about in the bottom of the boat.

People have been killed by piranhas, but in two years on South American rivers we never visited a place where the locals were afraid to swim and we never heard of anyone being attacked by them (though we did meet a man who'd had his finger bitten off by one while he was trying to get his fish hook out of its mouth). The stories of them congregating near riverbanks in huge shoals waiting to devour the flesh of anyone who dips a toe into the water are exaggerations of the reality; nevertheless, if local people warn you to take care because of the piranhas, heed their advice.

Piranhas are good to eat, the flesh being white and tender although rather bland and full of sharp little bones. Where they are abundant they are easy to catch with any kind of meat bait, but be careful: They don't die easily. Tanis once began to prepare one for the pot believing it to be dead when it suddenly started snapping its jaws together. This particular fish had been hooked, clubbed, and then left on dry land for six hours before she picked it up. Several related species of fish, superficially resembling piranhas, are vegetarian, and browse on river plants. These are the kind that are often shot with arrows by Amerindian people. (See Indian Fishing Methods, page 43)

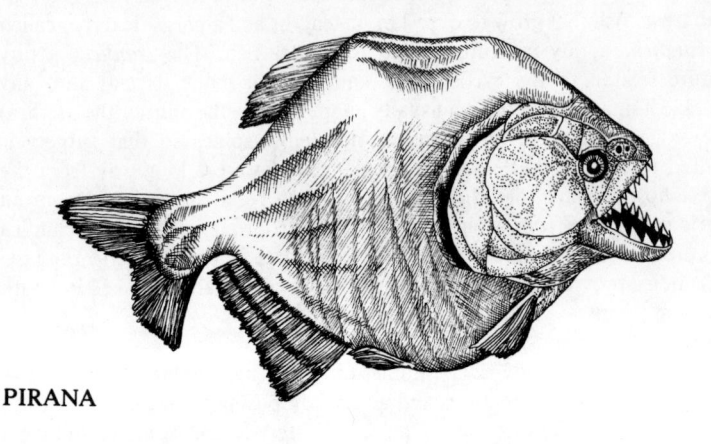

PIRANA

Electric eel.
These fish look like eels but are related to catfish. They grow up to 2 m. long and inhabit slow-moving waters, deep pools, and swamps, and are frequently observed because of their uncharacteristically fishlike habit of coming to the surface at regular intervals to breathe air. From the point of view of a person who simply wants to swim in a river, the most significant thing about these fascinating creatures is that a large specimen can produce an electric shock powerful enough to render a human being unconscious. Electric eels, though far less common than piranhas, have probably caused the deaths of more people.

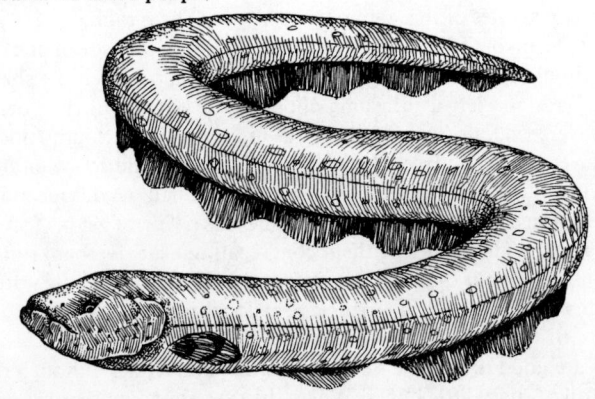

Electric eels can't see too well but find their way around by echo location in much the same way as do bats. The electrical discharge can vary in intensity, but a killer blow from a large fish can be in excess of 600 volts.

Stingray.
Very common in some places, stingrays are apparently absent from others. Lying in the shallows on the riverbed, they are impossible to see until they move, something they do with seemingly great reluctance. You may be informed, as we were, that stingrays are to be found only on sand, but don't believe it; we've come across them on sand, mud, gravel, and pebbles. If you're unfortunate enough to tread on one, it will lash you with its tail and puncture your flesh with its spine, set near the base of the tail. Traditionally, it was accepted that stingrays inject a venomous substance and that heat will help to inactivate this venom. More recently, it has been claimed that no venom is involved, merely a deep and jagged wound. Whichever you choose to believe, all accounts agree that a stingray's sting is excruciatingly painful, readily becomes infected, and can take months to heal. We once ran aground in our boat right on top of a stingray that measured a full meter across the "wings."

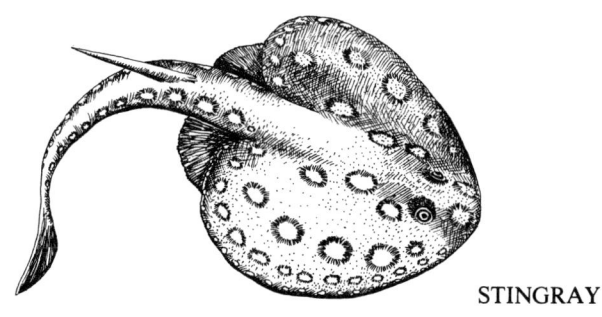

STINGRAY

Indian Fishing Methods

Shooting fish with arrows is particularly useful in the dry seasons when waters are shallow and clear and several large species are regularly found near the surface browsing on aquatic plants. The arrows used for this purpose are up to 2 m. long (see the cover painting) and are attached to the man by a cord that can be hauled in when the prey has been pierced. The only difficulty here is that an underwater object is not located where you seem to see it. This is a consequence of light refraction in the water. The arrow has to be aimed at a point below the apparent position of the fish in order to hit it.

Another method is to poison water. A liana of the genus paullinia *(also: pawlownia) is used for this purpose, the sap from which stupifies fish, causing them to float to the surface as if dead, though they may recover if released into unpolluted water. The first time we witnessed this event, the whole community was involved. One afternoon a man arrived in the village with two bundles of thin, woody vines. For the rest of that day, dozens of children sat on boulders at the riverside methodically pounding the vines with rocks, reducing them to a fibrous pulp. Before dawn the following day the whole village set forth to a spot where a creek had been dammed and a large still pool formed. The pulp was thrown onto the water and everyone began beating the surface with sticks. Soon, to yells of excitement, fish began to appear on the surface, some of them belly up, where they were quickly speared or clubbed to death. We returned to the village later that morning, every person carrying a kilo or more of fish. The rest of the day was spent in celebration, drinking cassiri and eating baked fish and cassava bread.*

I believe that the active ingredient of this liana is a neurotoxin that somehow affects the fish's ability to take up oxygen yet doesn't get into the flesh to poison the person who eats it.

Jungle Ecology

Jungles are the most ancient and complex vegetation systems on earth. It's from the tropics that all other land plants probably originated and spread, and it's in these torrid zones that nature is at her most extravagant; even the grass there can grow 10 m. high (bamboo). South America contains about one third of the world's trees and their diversity is mind-blowing. For example, 200 trees growing in a small area of virgin jungle in Guyana were made up of 120 different species! In practice, this situation makes it quite difficult to find two trees of the same species and you'd need to be a real expert to be able to put a name to one tree in twenty. Compare this to a forest in the higher latitudes of say, the United Kingdom or the United States where 200 forest trees would be made up of perhaps six or seven species.

But it's not just the plants that show this extraordinary diversity. Consider the birds: Some 3,000 species of birds live in the forests and mountains of South America. That's one third of the bird species in the entire world and five times the number found in the whole of Europe. There is a greater variety of living things per unit area of tropical rain forest than any other land environment.

Up in the trees the proliferation of leaves is arranged into several indistinct but recognizable layers at different heights above the ground. Each layer experiences different conditions of temperature, humidity, and light. Every species of tree at every level can be a special little environment suited to one or a whole group of living things, using or being used by others in some way. Imagine for a moment a colony of insects that can breed only in the waters that collect in the leaves of one particular type of plant. This plant can root itself in only one species of tree in the conditions found at a certain level. Now imagine a specialized tree frog that feeds almost exclusively on these insects. At this point let's introduce a lizard that regularly feeds on tree frogs and a bird that lives nearby because it favors these lizards as a dietary item, and so on until just about every plant and animal in the jungle has been mentioned. They all relate to each other in some way, however obscurely. This is vividly demonstrated by the indications that when one species of plant or animal is exterminated, a dozen others disappear as a direct or indirect consequence before equilibrium is once again restored.

The jungle is a place where modern man is still a stranger and where events continue in much the same way as they have for millions of years. Neither the ecology nor the global significance of this wilderness is understood except at the most rudimentary levels and maybe half of the things that live there have not been classified.

In recent years a quarter of the earth's jungles has been destroyed. Every minute of every day another 15 hectares (about 40 acres) falls under the axe and the rate of destruction is increasing. If it continues, there won't be much left in 30 years.

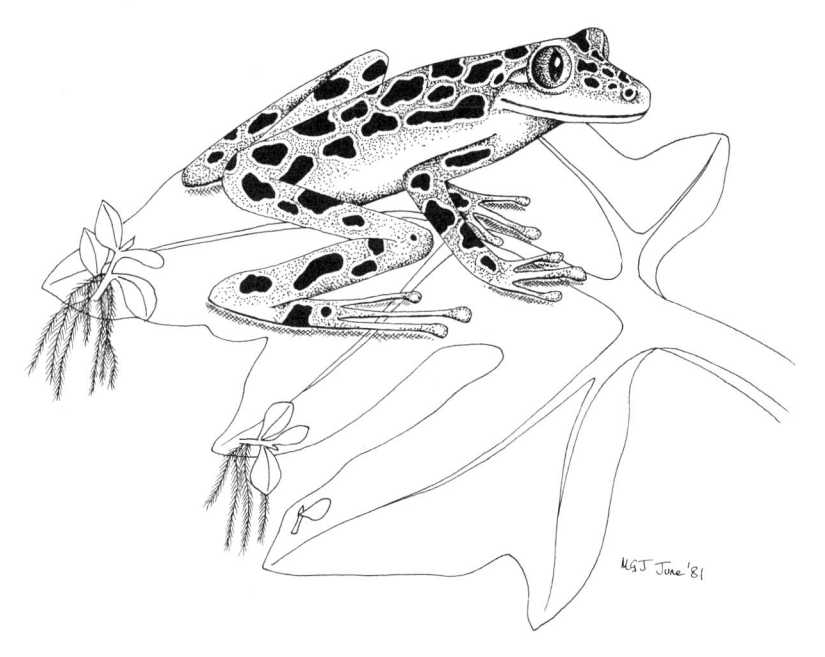

Arrow Poison Frog
Many species of brightly colored, conspicuously marked frogs live in the South American jungle. The skins of some of them contain powerful toxins that are used by Amerindian people for poisoned arrows and dart tips.

In the Jungle

The first time you step inside a tropical rain forest you find yourself in a cool, shady, quiet world, bathed in diffuse green light. You are surrounded by straight boles of high trees, ropelike vines, and bundles of knotty, twisted lianas dangling from high above, the branches from which they hang lost to view among the green chaos of leaves. The ground is dappled with sunlight but the leafy canopy is like a high ceiling and the place seems like an empty cathedral. Where, you wonder, are all the birds and beasts? Most of them are in the sunshine 40 m. or more above your head in the branches of those tall trees, along with the orchids and ferns and the other plants that grow up there. As for the big animals who walk the forest floor — the jaguars, tapirs, peccaries, and the like — if there were any in the vicinity when you arrived, they'll have wandered off before you spotted them.

It takes several days for your senses to become accustomed to this strange environment and then you begin to see more. First you notice the conspicuous things: big blue butterflies, lizards and frogs, parrots and toucans. As you become fascinated by the jungle, you may want to spend some time living in it. If you do, you'll soon become familiar with the shier creatures, too: ocelots, armadillos, deer, anteaters, snakes, and others too numerous to mention. By that time you'll have come to realize that the rain forest, which at first seemed an empty, brooding, surrealistic world of elegant and grotesque shapes and untraceable sounds is in reality one of the liveliest places on earth.

In the forest you may well hear an animal before you see it. Stand still and look around without moving your head too quickly; chances are that whatever made the sound will also be quite still and looking right at you.

Troupes of monkeys often create a considerable disturbance in the high branches. They'll cease their activities and move off if they spot you (they might even throw things at you). If you walk among the trees to get a better view of them, take care not to lose your way.

Seeing the larger animals like jaguar, tapir, and deer is largely a matter of luck. You'll greatly increase your chances if you're prepared to get up and go out at dawn. Tracks on riverbanks can tell a great deal about the local animal population. This is particularly true of the dry season when many small streams have dried out and animals come down to the larger tributaries and main rivers. In soft mud and sand tracks will be most conspicuous.

Some animals whose tracks are likely to be found in riverside sand or mud are shown below. With the exception of birds, insects, and lizards, these tracks are usually made at night, dusk, and dawn.

THE LIMA TIMES

Peru's English Language Weekly
Articles on mountaineering and exploration.
Carabaya 928 - 304, Lima

SQUIRREL MONKEY

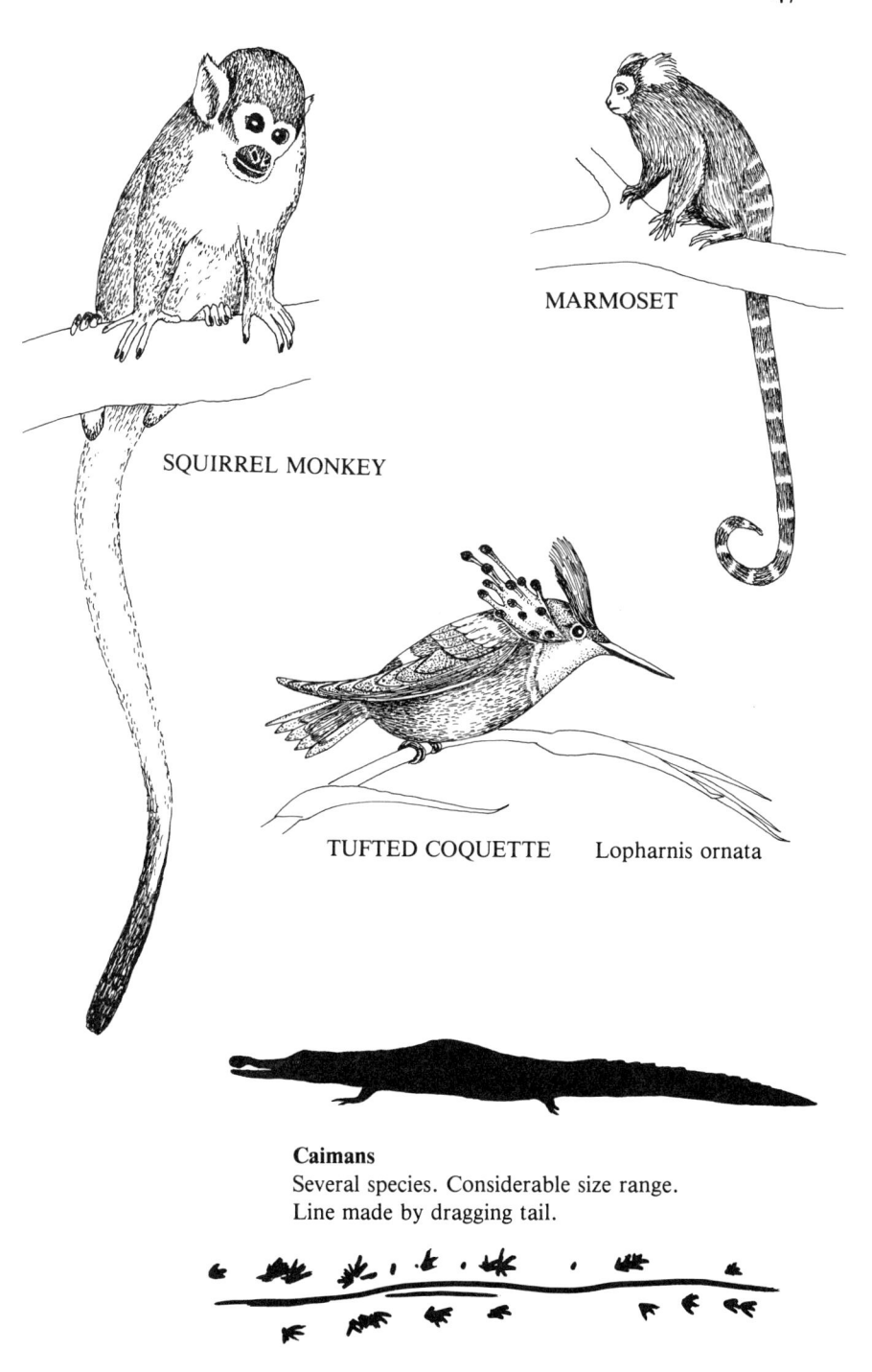

MARMOSET

TUFTED COQUETTE Lopharnis ornata

Caimans
Several species. Considerable size range.
Line made by dragging tail.

Jungle Sounds

At times the jungle is a noisy place. The dawn and dusk chorus of birds, frogs, and insects can drown conversation, and some of the sounds they make are just plain weird. In Surinam there's a little frog that screams "Who are you? Who are you?" over and over in a harsh, high-pitched, metallic voice. At night another frog hops around the forest floor saying "Ho, Ho, Ho," in rich deep tones.

Cicadas are noisy insects wherever found, but in the Venezuelan highlands live very large ones and you must actually hear them to believe the volume of sound they produce. When they start up just before sunset, the noise resembles the whine of circular saws and it has you putting your fingers in your ears.

Of course, I mustn't forget the mammals. The most vocally impressive are the howler monkeys. Their voice amplification system enables them to make a noise louder than that made by any other creature — louder even than the roar of a lion or the trumpeting of an elephant! At a distance the sound is like a wailing wind, at close range it's a booming roar.

But apart from all the recognizable sounds — the whistles, shrieks, howls, grunts, chimes, yells, and cries — there are unexpected sounds that have no imaginable natural origin. You may hear somebody banging a tin bucket with a stick, or a random sequence of notes played on a violin, a sudden burst of insane laughter, the whistle of a train. These unexplainable sounds have a place in the folklore of the indigenous forest people who should know the jungle's inhabitants better than anyone. They believe them to be voices from the spirit world.

At night, sounds take on added significance. Along with the familiar hoots of owls and chirrups of crickets are a host of unfamiliar clicks, hisses, and isolated screams. After heavy rain, mighty trees collapse with thunderous crashes, a sound you never notice during the day but may hear half a dozen times in a single night. One night a tree fell near our camp. The noise was so great and the ground shook to such an extent that we thought it had almost fallen on top of us and we never slept again that night. In the morning we searched but could not find a fallen tree; it had come down at least 300 m. away.

By a remote river in southeast Peru we made camp one afternoon knowing that we were in country frequented by groups of uncontacted Indians. No sooner had we erected the tent than a loud regular knocking started from nearby. It was like a drum being struck at ten-second intervals. For half an hour we listened to it with rising anxiety until, unable to bear the suspense any longer, we felt compelled to go into the forest and discover who or what was doing it. (Our speculations had led us to believe that it was a wild Indian beating a hollow tree with a stick to summon all the other Indians in the region to inform them of our arrival.)

After ten minutes of creeping through the woods, hearts in mouths, expecting at any moment a volley of arrows or poison darts, the sound drew us to a tall, dead hollow tree. Halfway up it was a big chestnut-colored

TOUCAN

SPIDER MONKEY

RED FAN PARROT

CAPUCHIN MONKEY

woodpecker that looked down at us quizzically before turning its attention to the task in hand: Slowly it drew back its head, waited for a count of five then struck the tree a resounding blow. Unidentifiable sounds in lonely jungles provide wonderful exercise for active imaginations.

Creek Drifting

A great way to see animals is to drift on the water after dark. An hour or so after sunset is the best time to go. Allow your boat to drift passively with the current 3 or 4 m. from the riverbank, steering gently with a paddle. Carry a good flashlight (check that the beam doesn't have a shadow in the center) and direct the beam onto the sandbars and among the trees. The light will be reflected back from the interior of animals' eyes as a red glow, like burning coals. Keep the flashlight positioned near your head so that the reflected light from their eyes comes right back to yours. This is so effective that with a strong beam it's possible to see the eyes of a small lizard at 10 m. or more.

When creek drifting you stand a fair chance of seeing the big cats, tapir, and the like. Shine the beam into the water and you'll see huge fish that are not about in the daylight hours. In the shallows you'll see caimans. Three things to beware of and the first two are rather obvious: Don't allow yourself to drift passively over the rim of a waterfall. Don't get lost; make sure you can identify your campsite when you return. The third hazard concerns the wild animals. Don't get too close to caimans, especially big ones; they really do attack boats at times. Peccaries can be aggressive and sometimes appear in large bands of hundreds of individuals. We were once in a boat and came upon twenty or more peccaries swimming across a river (though this was daytime). We pulled up close to take photos and the whole lot turned on us in united attack and we had to flee.

River Gold

Finding gold in known gold-bearing rivers (and there are a great many such rivers in South America) is a simple matter. Take some of the silt, sand, and gravel mixture from the streambed, spread it across a flat surface, and splash water on it. You'll see tiny glittering flecks here and there. The silvery ones will be worthless mica, but with any luck there'll be yellow ones too, and they will be gold.

Of course, discovering minute quantities, barely visible to the naked eye, is a lot easier than extracting large amounts of the stuff. The oldest and simplest method makes use of a wide, shallow pan. Into this you put a shovel full of stony riverbed material and water, and swish it round in a circular motion on a horizontal plane in such a manner that the least dense material (mud, yellow sand, and stones) slops over the edge of the pan while the most dense material (black sand and gold) falls to the middle. The gold dust is removed from the sand by kneading the whole lot with a little mercury. This amalgamates with the gold into larger particles that are more easily removed. Finally the mercury is burned off, leaving a little blob of pure gold.

At this point comes a warning about the dangers associated with this particular occupation. Whatever you do, don't just go out and begin working a riverbed. You could be panning on somebody else's claim, thus running the risk of being murdered. Alternatively you could find yourself in serious trouble with the law. If you want to search for gold (or platinum or gems), make your desire known to the authorities. And if you do give it a try, make sure you don't inhale any mercury vapor in the final stage of the operation; it's one of the most lethal gases known.

There's a lot of money in gold extraction and modern methods are on a fittingly large scale, involving the total destruction of areas of land by explosives and diversion of rivers. Nevertheless, what you still see most of out in the backwoods is people standing in the water panning, or washing gravel down homemade wooden canals.

Will you wind up wealthy if you give it a try? Well, what cannot be denied is that all the gold that's scattered thinly throughout those endless rivers comes from source areas in the ground that must be vast. Gold particles are worn smaller and smaller as they are transported farther from their point of origin so if you start finding gold nuggets weighing half a kilogram each, you'll know that you're pretty close to the fabled golden land of El Dorado. Find that, and you'll never again need to worry about how much it will cost to make a South American river trip.

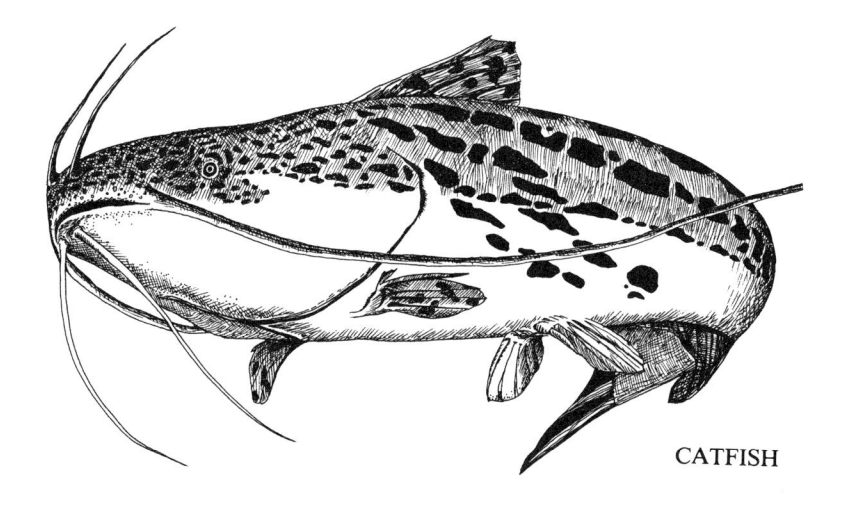

CATFISH

MAP NUMBER 1

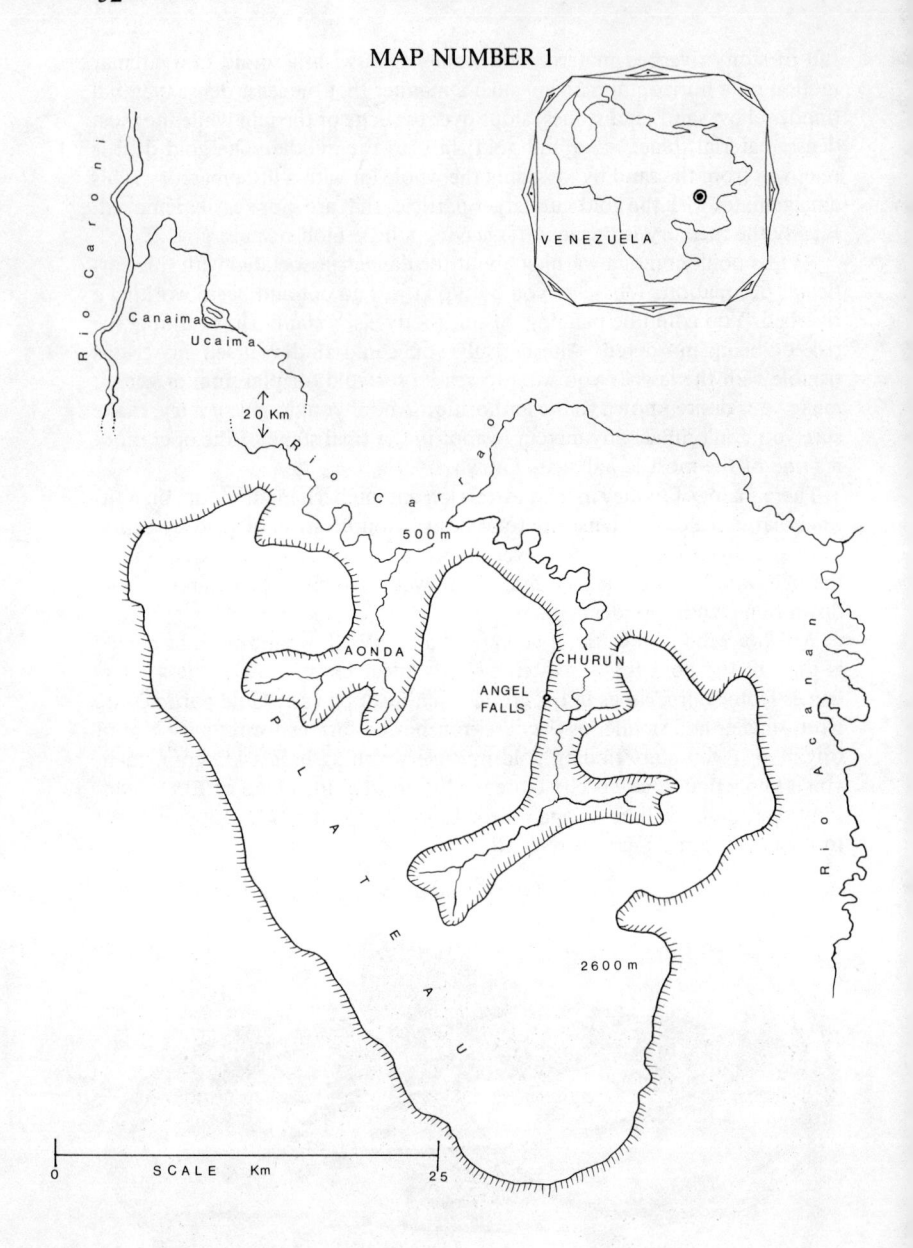

Venezuela

Canaima National Park

Canaima Park can be reached only by air; regular flights are available from Caracas, via Ciudad Bolivar, by AVENSA National Airlines. There are two tourist camps in the park, in the middle of a vast, mountainous jungle wilderness containing some of the most staggeringly spectacular scenery imaginable. A government camp called Canaima is set beside a wide lagoon beneath a horseshoe of beautiful waterails, the Hacha Falls. The natural setting is delightful but there are scores of little chalets, bars, and a restaurant and the area is expensive, noisy, and littered with trash. You may find yourself in the company of the worst kind of tourists, those loud travelers of every nationality who require air-conditioned luxury and are indifferent to everything but waiter service and good food. We met a group that had spent the day picking orchids — in a national park!

But . . . a jungle trail leads up from Canaima to another camp called Ucaima, above the Hacha Falls. This is run by Rudy and Gerti Truffino. Jungle Rudy, the official park guard and guide, was exploring this part of Venezuela before the maps were made. Nobody knows more about the area than does he. The camp has an airstrip for light aircraft, a dozen or more bungalows to let, a bar, and good food. Rudy shows films of the area in the evenings.

Excursions can be arranged from both camps but be warned: Organized trips are of short duration and are very expensive. In the rainy season (June to December) there are occasional four- to six-day canoe expeditions to Angel Falls where you can hike through the jungle to the base of the 1,000-m.high waterfall, an experience that will remove from your mind all worries about how much the trip is costing. Both Ucaima and Canaima have offices in Caracas where arrangements can be made.

If you wish to take your own boat and go exploring in the Canaima National Park, you'll have to apply for permission from the Ministry of

Agriculture in Caracas. No gas is available at either camp unless prior arrangements are made. Food is not on sale openly, but either camp may be willing to sell to you; again, make prior arrangements. Beer is available at both camps. All equipment can be flown out to Canaima by AVENSA. Rudy has a four-wheel drive vehicle, and there is a track between the camps. Light aircraft sometimes fly down to both camps, so it may be possible to get a lift into the park.

It's also possible to mount an expedition from the Camarata mission many miles upriver of Auyantepui (the mountain from which Angel Falls descends), but we have no firsthand experience with this. On the Carrao River just above Ucaima are severe rapids (called Mayupa) that continue upriver; after these are several smaller sets of rapids, that continue until you turn into the Churun Canyon on the Churn River, which flows past Angel Falls. On this river there are scores of rapids of varying degrees of severity. In the dry season it's possible to haul up some and portage around others.

Carrao River and Aonda Canyon

Table mountains dot the plains of the highlands of northern South America from Colombia eastward to French Guiana and south into Brazil. These mesas or tepuis are remnants of a vast sandstone plateau that once covered the whole region, the bed of an ancient ocean laid down before there were dinosaurs or even land plants and then lifted by crustal readjustment to be whittled away by the weather. Some of the oldest rocks in the world are found here.

Auyantepui is the largest of the tepuis. Its flat summit, some 900 km.^{2} in area, is covered with swamps and forest and isolated from the steaming jungle by sheer rugged cliffs. The mountain acts as a gigantic condenser of atmospheric water and the enormous rainfall it receives drains off into two canyons in the northern side. Angel Falls, the highest waterfall in the world, drops for 1 km. over the vertical rock face into one of these canyons, the Churun. This waterfall was discovered in 1935 by an Amercian adventurer named Jimmy Angel.

On a morning in late January we climbed aboard our inflatable rubber boat, started the 6-h.p. engine, and set off up the Carrao River. Our plan was to spend a month exploring the Aonda Canyon before heading farther upstream to Angel Falls. The boat was so overloaded that we were forced to sit perched on top of piles of equipment with our feet on the tubes and we made such slow progress that it was fifteen minutes before we were out of sight of the assemblage of people on the riverbank who had come to see us off! It became quite embarrassing and our faces and arms ached from the effort of smiling and waving for so long. Our intention, to travel the river for about four months, already seemed in doubt. We began to wonder if we would make it up the first set of rapids, let alone as far as the distant hulk of Auyantepui.

The Table Mountain Auyantepui, Venezuela.

By mid-morning the mountains, blue and misty with distance, had gathered crowns of wispy cloud. On our own at last we pulled onto a beach of golden sand to take in our surroundings. From far away in the forest came the eerie wailing roar of a troupe of howler monkeys. Along the water's edge were clusters of green, yellow, and orange butterflies that resembled piles of confetti, all sucking at the wet sand. Kingfishers darted across the water's surface and a hummingbird hovered for a moment in front of our faces, more like some large, brilliant insect than a bird.

The Carrao River is crystal clear but tinted deep amber by humic acids leached from the vegetation. In the shallows where the sandy, pebbly bottom can be seen, the water looks like wine. At regular intervals along its length the river's meandering tranquility is broken by cataracts where foaming white water tumbles over rocky ledges and rushes between boulders. At the first turbulent stretch we motored up to a point where the current flowed too fast to make further progress and here I climbed out onto a flat rock and held the boat steady by means of a long painter (a rope tied to the prow). Tanis got into the water and pushed the boat while I pulled the rope and in this way we moved slowly upstream. It was difficult to maintain balance when the water was only knee deep and at anything greater than that depth it was impossible to move forward. We couldn't communicate with each other verbally because the roar of the water was too loud and at one point I looked back to see Tanis suspended in an almost horizontal position above the water with her feet on a rock and her hands on the boat. She was shouting words I couldn't hear, though clearly the message was for me to stop pulling. Too late. She fell with a splash and reappeared, swimming for the bank downstream. Twice I slid over on the slippery rocks and let go of the rope so the boat, with Tanis clinging to the side of it, was carried away by the current. It took us two hours to get above those rapids, and if anyone had been watching us, he or she would have had the laugh of a lifetime. Despite this, when we finally reached quiet water we were pleased with ourselves. We'd managed the operation without losing or damaging anything and we could only get better with practice. In the months that followed we got ourselves up three rivers and over a hundred sets of rapids by this means and by portages (carrying everthing around the really heavy rapids) without a single serious mishap.

The mouth of the Aonda Canyon is about 4 km. wide and accessible via a small, rocky stream that empties into the Carrao. From the riverbank the jungle-covered valley climbs to the foot of lofty turretted cliffs. After rain, ephemeral waterfalls cascade down the vertical rock face in silver streams hundreds of meters high, then dry up only hours later. At night in our tent we heard the rumble of distant rockfalls, a sound distinguishable from thunder by the vibration of the ground under us.

We'd been assured that were we to stay in the Aonda Canyon for years we'd meet no other people, yet one day we saw a thin column of smoke rising high above the trees in the still air. It was surprising how much of a shock this gave us. Tanis remained with the boat and I set off into the jungle to find out who it was.

For the next ten minutes I pushed my way past bushes and vines and eventually emerged into the sunlight of a man-made clearing some 15 m. across. In the center was a pile of burning timber. Beyond this among the trees I could see a large, gray canvas sheet, strung up as a shelter over somebody's living quarters. Most surprising of all was the resident, a bearded, completely naked white man, kneeling on the ground and apparently engaged in gardening.

"Buenos dias," I called and he jumped to his feet and stood staring at me. He looked about fifty years old, muscular and tanned a deep golden brown as if it were his habit to work naked in the sun. Hanging from a string around his neck was a pair of spectacles and he put them on to see me better. We walked toward one another and shook hands.

"You American?" he inquired.

"No, English," I replied.

"Come with me, I show you something," he ordered in a heavy accent that did not sound Spanish. He led me to where he had been kneeling when I first saw him and showed me tomato plants, explaining sadly that he did not hold out much hope that they would ever reach maturity.

"Just an experiment," he added, shrugging his shoulders. We strolled over to the canvas shelter. Beneath it was a long table constructed from poles and lashed together with vines, Indian fashion. Upon it were the utensils and provisions one would expect to see in a jungle camp and in addition there was a large number of books in a variety of languages. One that particularly caught my eye was *The Naked Ape* by Desmond Morris. Obviously the man was no Robinson Crusoe stranded in the wilds. After five minutes chatting about such topics as the weather and the number of tourists at Canaima, he went back to his tomato patch and continued his work. I took this as my cue to leave, but the meeting had been most unsatisfactory from my point of view. I'd learned nothing at all about him. Direct questions to strangers can easily and justifiably cause offense, but I felt compelled to risk a couple.

"Where do you come from?" I asked.

"Latvia," he replied.

"Have you been here long?" I continued, encouraged by his ready response.

"About fifteen years."

There followed a moments silence while I absorbed this information, then I said, "OK, I'll be off now. Goodbye."

"Goodbye."

I walked back through the jungle, wondering if Tanis was going to believe this.

The following weeks went by almost too quickly for us. Our days were spent walking in the forest, climbing in the hills, following the partially dried up riverbed or sometimes just swimming and sunbathing. Regularly we saw peccaries, tapir, and sometimes jaguars. There were few monkeys in the forests; we glimpsed only one troupe of red howlers during our stay there. At the eastern end of the canyon we made a sinister discovery: several pieces of airplane fuselage that we reckoned had been there for many years. We searched all day for a wreck but found nothing. One night there was a violent storm followed by a flash flood. A wall of water 2 m. high came thundering down the little rocky stream carrying away all in its path, a dramatic reminder of the unpredictability of highland rivers. Anyone camping on the beach that night would probably have been killed.

On our way out of the canyon near the main river, the Latvian was waiting on the riverbank dressed this time in shirt, shorts, and Wellington boots. He explained that he had been worried because we'd been away for so long and was glad to see us safe and well. He'd been considering coming to search for us.

"By the way," he inquired casually, "did you find any gold?"

So that was it. He'd spent the last few weeks trying to figure out what we'd been doing in there. I replied truthfully, "No. We didn't even look for any."

Churun Canyon and Angel Falls

Back at the Carrao we made camp for a few days before entering the river that drains Auyantepui's second and much larger canyon, Churun Canyon. It was here that Martin decided to try his hand at fishing, with almost immediate success. I was cleaning up in the tent when I heard him calling me and rushed outside to find him holding aloft on the fishing line a 5 or 6 kg. specimen of *aimara*, a bottom-dwelling fish with an even more fearsome set of teeth than the dreaded piranha.

"Get the camera," he said excitedly, and laid his catch on the sand. Then an astonishing thing happened. With a convulsive jerk the fish slipped the hook, turned around and methodically began making its way down to the river, 10 m. distant. It moved by writhing its body from side to side like a drunken snake.

"Quick, Tanis, it's escaping!" shouted Martin, grabbing at it with both hands. Its grizzly head twisted sideways, teeth snapping viciously, and Martin dropped it. Seconds later the aimara reached the water and was gone. No fish steaks for us that night.

On the next day we set off toward the Churun Canyon. The winding river that flows from it is steep and rocky with rapids at regular intervals. Toiling up this river, often by dragging the boat across the rocks, was backbreaking work but the scenery was grand: massive cliffs, pink and mauve in the sunlight, with higher waterfalls than we had yet seen, some falling from the rim of the plateau and others issuing from fissures lower down.

Between the rapids lay stretches of still water, in places so calm that the surface was littered with a fine debris of dead leaves and dust lying there as if on a sheet of glass. Iridescent hummingbirds hovered and darted among the flowers that grew at the forest's edge and large numbers of kingfishers congregated around these quiet pools. In one place we counted fourteen of them, representing at least three different species. They would fly down to catch the little fish disturbed by the passage of our boat.

Serpents lived in our garden of Eden as well. One day we stopped for a rest on a sandbank and Martin took a stroll along the riverside. I was watching him absentmindedly when he suddenly leapt into the air like a professional ballet dancer. He'd almost trodden on a rattlesnake, which reared up at him but fortunately did not strike.

On the morning of our fifth day in the canyon we rounded a bend in the river and there in the distance was Angel Falls. My first impression was that the water seemed to be falling too slowly. In its 1,000-m. drop the stream broke up and tumbled over and over, twisting and spiraling rather like a plume of smoke traveling straight down instead of up. The water took so long to make the descent that Angel Falls seemed slightly unreal, like a film shown in slow motion.

Nothing man-made can be found near Angel Falls except a stone cabin on the north bank of the Churun River used by occasional expedition parties during the rainy season. There's nothing to detract from the remote wildness of the place. A walker's trail through damp and silent forest leads to the Angel River, which runs down from the falls. We crossed the river on a convenient fallen tree, and after a steep and tiring climb emerged unexpectedly from the shelter of the trees onto a high rocky outcrop to be confronted by a breathtaking sight: a vertical river of water only 200 m. from where we stood, its top lost in the clouds. Below, the lush forest ended abruptly at the edge of a barren field littered with jagged boulders onto which the water fell, exploding into a huge cloud of mist and spray. It wasn't nearly as noisy as we'd expected, but there was a strong wind that carried the fine drizzle over us, and we were soon soaking wet. We had seen photographs of the falls but we were not prepared for the reality of standing almost underneath it. It's just not possible to visualize a waterfall over 1 km. high. A series of smaller falls disappeared down into the jungle below us, forming the Angel River. Somewhere on this planet there might be a more spectacular sight then the Angel Falls, but frankly, I doubt it.

We had been told that there could be a waterfall even higher than the Angel Falls much deeper in the Canyon. Certainly it seemed a possibility to us. The Churun River is not even noticeably enlarged by the output of Angel Falls, meaning that vast quantities of water are entering the drainage system higher upstream. Also, the higher end of the canyon is almost always clouded over and turbulent air makes it impossible for pilots to fly in and take a look at what's up there without risking a crash. We packed some food and set off deeper into the canyon on foot. The river was too fierce and rocky to take the boat.

Well, we didn't discover the world's highest waterfall, but what we did find was a truly terrifying environment where jungle grew over the tops of huge boulders, the yawning chasms separating them spanned by networks of matted roots. Down these gaps between the rocks we could not always see the ground and in places could hear the roar of rushing water far below. Martin was ahead of me cutting a trail when suddenly he fell back, hurling down his machete and tearing off his shirt. My first thought was snakebite, but I knew he wasn't foolish enough to jump about like that if he'd been bitten. But what else could cause such frenzy?

"I've hit an ants' nest!" Martin shouted back to me.

Of course! I was glad he was busily occupied because I was falling about with laughter at the sight of him frantically slapping himself in a vain attempt to rid himself of the hundreds of red ants on his naked chest and back. The day before I had been taking a compass reading when an agonizing pain shot up my leg. I had inadvertently been standing for some time over the opening of an ants' nest and when I moved my foot a large number of them took their revenge on me for depriving them of air. I jumped about in a panic trying to keep them from getting past my knees and only when I was winning the battle did I realize that I had dropped the camera bag. It had rolled down a slope and was wedged against a boulder halfway over the edge of a cavernous hole. We were able to retrieve it, but I had to put up with a lecture about being more careful with the equipment. Now, as his machete was nowhere in sight and his shirt was hanging way up in a tree, the tables were turned, but he was so covered with bites I didn't have the heart to make my point about carefulness.

We turned back after three days when we became thoroughly fed up with the expedition making no progress, just wandering in any direction that allowed us to get from one boulder to another.

One morning, back at our camp near Angel Falls, we awoke to the sound of heavy rain beating down on the tent. Twenty-four hours later it was still raining and the Churun River had risen by 4 m. and was now an unrecognizable raging torrent transporting huge tree trunks past our door at frightening speed. Another day passed and it was still pouring. The rainy season had arrived.

We waited for two more days during which time the rain eased and the river dropped a meter or so and then we decided to test the boat and engine against the current to determine what degree of control we would have on the downstream journey. Keeping near the bank we made our way about 15 m. upstream but as we nosed carefully into the fast current midstream, the boat began to swing around and at that moment the engine cut out. Before Martin could start it again we began drifting backward at quite a speed. Bushes and trees shot by at an alarming pace and I clutched wildly at them in an attempt to slow down the boat. When I saw the camp go by I panicked and grabbed a branch with both hands. The next thing I knew I was hanging waist deep in water and slowly sinking as the branch gave with my weight. The only good thing was that my action had slowed the boat enough for Martin to bring it to a halt, but I hung there for ages before he could stop laughing long enough to rescue me.

We left the next day and once we committed ourselves to the river we were out of the canyon in only half a day, swept along at a tremendous pace and using the engine only to steer us out of trouble. We passed great flocks of waterfowl that had flown in with the rains. No dry land was now visible; in places the waters had risen above the banks and the jungle appeared to be growing out of the river. Drifting along, we watched a long-legged hawk swoop from the sky and pluck a thin green snake out of a tree. The bird then settled on a branch overhanging the water with the now dead snake grasped in its talons but as we floated past the bird took flight and dropped its prey in the water.

Angel Falls, Venezuela

MAP NUMBER 2

Surinam

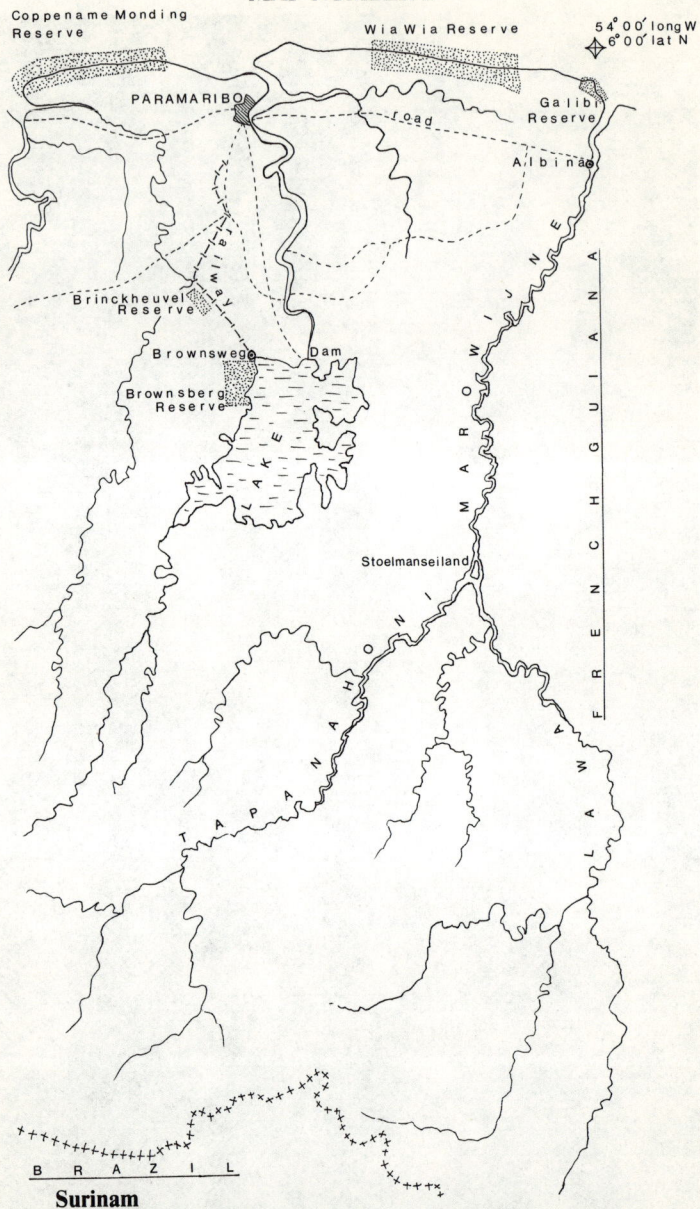

Map of Surinam showing nature reserves described in text. It's possible to cross the Marowijne River from Albina to St. Laurent, visit the old prison of Papillon fame, and enjoy some good French cuisine. Because of border disputes with neighboring Guyana, it's inadvisable to travel on the Courantyne River.

Surinam

Wildlife Conservation

Surinam has an energetic and extremely well organized conservation body called STINASU (Foundation for Nature Preservation). They can be reached at Corn Jongbawstr. 14, P.O. Box 436, Paramaribo; telephone 71856 or 75845 - 37. From their headquarters in Paramaribo it's possible to arrange trips to the country's parks and reserves. Surinam has both easily accessible areas with comfortable accommodations and several huge, uninhabited virgin forest reserves. In the least accessible regions, human beings are such rare intruders that wild animals are relatively bold and easily observed. On the coast over 100 km. of uninhabited beaches provide some of the most important breeding grounds in the world for many species of marine turtles. From here it is possible to travel up the tidal creeks into the swamps where the bird life is wonderfully prolific and varied.

NOTE: Surinam is a sparsely populated country with perhaps as much as 80 percent of it virtually uninhabited and covered by tropical rain forest. Because there are few roads except in the the coastal regions, getting to remote areas can be both time-consuming and costly. As a consequence, organized trips are not cheap; in our opinion however, the best value for the money is obtained from STINASU.

Climate. There are two dry seasons, a short one in February and March and a long one from early August through November.

Coastal Nature Reserves

There are three coastal reserves, Coppename Monding, Wia Wia, and Galibi, and there is a STINASU lodge at Matapica (see map for locations). Asscess to Wia Wia and Galibi is strictly controlled between February and July when the turtles come ashore to lay eggs and this is, of course, the very best time to visit. Carib Indians live near Galibi and the men go to sea on fishing expeditions using traditional sail-driven vessels, a unique innovation among South American Indians.

All three reserves have lodges to accommodate guests. None of the areas can be visited without making arrangements with STINASU and the cost of transport will be the most expensive item for a short stay. For example, to visit Galibi a boat from Albina taking up to six persons will cost $65 round trip, and a bed at the lodge $2.50 (1981 U.S. prices).

Forest Nature Reserves

Brinkheuval Reserve.
This area of savannah and rain forest was once a relatively populous gold-mining center though it's now uninhabited. It can be reached from Paramaribo, one hour by road and three hours on the slow, romatic Gold Train, a relic from the gold rush of early in this century. There are no accommodations at the reserve but it's possible to stay at the nearby village of Kwakoegron.

Tafelberg and Eilerts de Haan Reserves.
These are two vast, uninhabited, and largely unexplored regions, the former containing a table mountain of the Roraima formation. Next to nothing is known about their flora, fauna, ecology, geology, or anything else. Only properly equipped expeditions can penetrate these areas. If you decide to go, we'd be very interested to hear about your trip.

Sipaliwini Savannah (Proposed Reserve).
This wilderness area of tropical rain forest and open savannah extends to the Brazilian border and is uninhabited except by small groups of nomadic Trios Indians. Stone Age artifacts and settlements of early man abound in the area. Like the two reserves just described, this is not for the casual visitor.

PECCARY   CAPYBARA

Brownsberg Nature Park

If you've never before set foot inside a tropical jungle and are anxious to discover if it's the sort of environment that will fill your being with mystical peace or give you dark visions and nightmares, the place to go for an enlightening introduction is Brownsberg Nature Park.

This is an 8,500-hectare, forest-clad area beside the huge Brokopondo Reservoir, a lake created when the Afobaka Dam was closed on the Surinam River in 1964 inundating over 2,000 km.² of jungle. At that time a joint American/Surinamese team undertook the largest animal rescue operation ever, the subject of a splendid book called *Time Is Short and the Water Rises* (see bibliography).

Brownsberg has the tremendous advantage of being easily accessible. From Paramaribo you can get there by public bus, by ancient wood-burning steam train (see description of Brinkheuval Reserve), or privately by car or truck, arranged with STINASU. More precisely, the public transport will take you to a Bush Negro village called Brownsweg where you can hire a car or walk up a road cut through virgin jungle (be warned: it's a fairly stiff hike) to the Brownsberg camp on top of the Mazaroni Plateau. The camp contains bungalows where guests can stay in relative luxury, lodges where you can sling a hammock for a modest fee, or it's possible to pitch a tent. Make arrangements with STINASU before you visit.

From the plateau are marvelous views of the lake 500 m. below. Many forest trails lead to creeks and waterfalls and guides are available if you lack the confidence to walk alone. In fact, it's a good idea to have a guide along if you are new to the jungle because he will point out things that you would not otherwise notice.

The hillside forests are magnificent with very tall trees and in many places the ground between them is as open as in temperate woodland. Both temperature and humidity are lower than in the lowland forests and there are fewer biting insects. Bird life is prolific with many kinds of hummingbirds, parrots, and toucans and specialties like the large gray-winged trumpeter and the black curassow. Near the camp we discovered the most bizarre, exotic leaf insects that we've ever seen.

For observing birds and butterflies, hiking, and swimming (there are creeks with clear water and no dangerous fish), the dry season is the best time to go. To see mammals and reptiles it's better to go in the rainy season when they move away from the low-lying rivers to higher ground. In one week at Brownsberg during June (a very wet month when mud and puddles are everywhere) we saw five species of monkeys, brocket (red deer), peccaries, agouties, tortoises, armadillos, a tree porcupine, a tree anteater (tamandua), an ocelot, a puma, and between fifty and sixty snakes! We were also rudely awakened at dawn more than once by troupes of howler monkeys that came right through the camp roaring and wailing like banshees — a very eerie experience. That's a pretty good selection of creatures to see during one week in a South American tropical rain forest. When we returned for a week in September (a very dry month) we saw no snakes at all, very few mammals except monkeys, but far more birds. Verdict: It's a great place to visit any time of the year. Don't leave Surinam without making a trip to Brownsberg.

Raleigh Falls/Voltzberg Reserve

This reserve consists of 56,000 hectares (140,000 acres) on the Upper Coppename River. The landing strip, headquarters, and tourist lodges are on Foengoe Island. The park is a superb place for bird-watching and parties come from Europe and America specifically for this purpose. This wild area is uninhabited and beyond a few jungle trails remains unvisited. If you feel sufficiently adventurous to travel away from the regularly visited areas, you will have to apply for special permission from STINASU (after all, it's they who would be obligated to come out searching for you if you disappeared).

Three of us made the trip to the Raleigh Falls reserve: Tanis and I and my brother Dominic, who was on his first visit to South America and about to undertake his first canoe trip. Our starting point was a Bush Negro village called Bitagron on the east bank of the Coppename River, which is served by a good unsurfaced road. We had traveled from Paramaribo by truck, spent the night in a hut in the village, and by 10 A.M. were almost ready to leave.

The scene: Our canoe, tied to a tree trunk, floated on the brown water with me sitting in it. Tanis and Dom watched from the top of a very steep muddy bank that sloped down to the river at an angle of 70 degrees. Tanis was telling Dom about some of the dangerous fish to be found in the river, particularly piranhas, which are abundant in the Coppename. Suddenly an amazing thing happened: Tanis and Dom began sliding slowly down the bank toward the water, still in upright sitting positions but unable to stop themselves as they grabbed at twigs and roots that came away in their hands. It was as if they had wheels on their butts. About three quarters of the way down, Tanis came to a halt but Dom continued and disappeared with a splash into the murky depths. He surfaced, looked around, then struck out for the canoe like Mark Spitz going for gold. With Tanis's blood-thirsty descriptions still in his mind he was under the impression that within the next few seconds he was going to be stripped to the bone by piranha fish. He grabbed the side of the canoe and began hauling himself inside while I, convinced that he would capsize us, put my hand on his head and began forcing him back into the water. For a few moments we were locked in a desperate struggle that to Dom, seemed like a matter of life or death until some mutual understanding was regained and I paddled the canoe to the bank with my brother clinging to the side. The incident had been witnessed by an appreciative audience of a dozen village folk who enjoyed it so much they were still busting their sides half an hour later.

MAP NUMBER 3

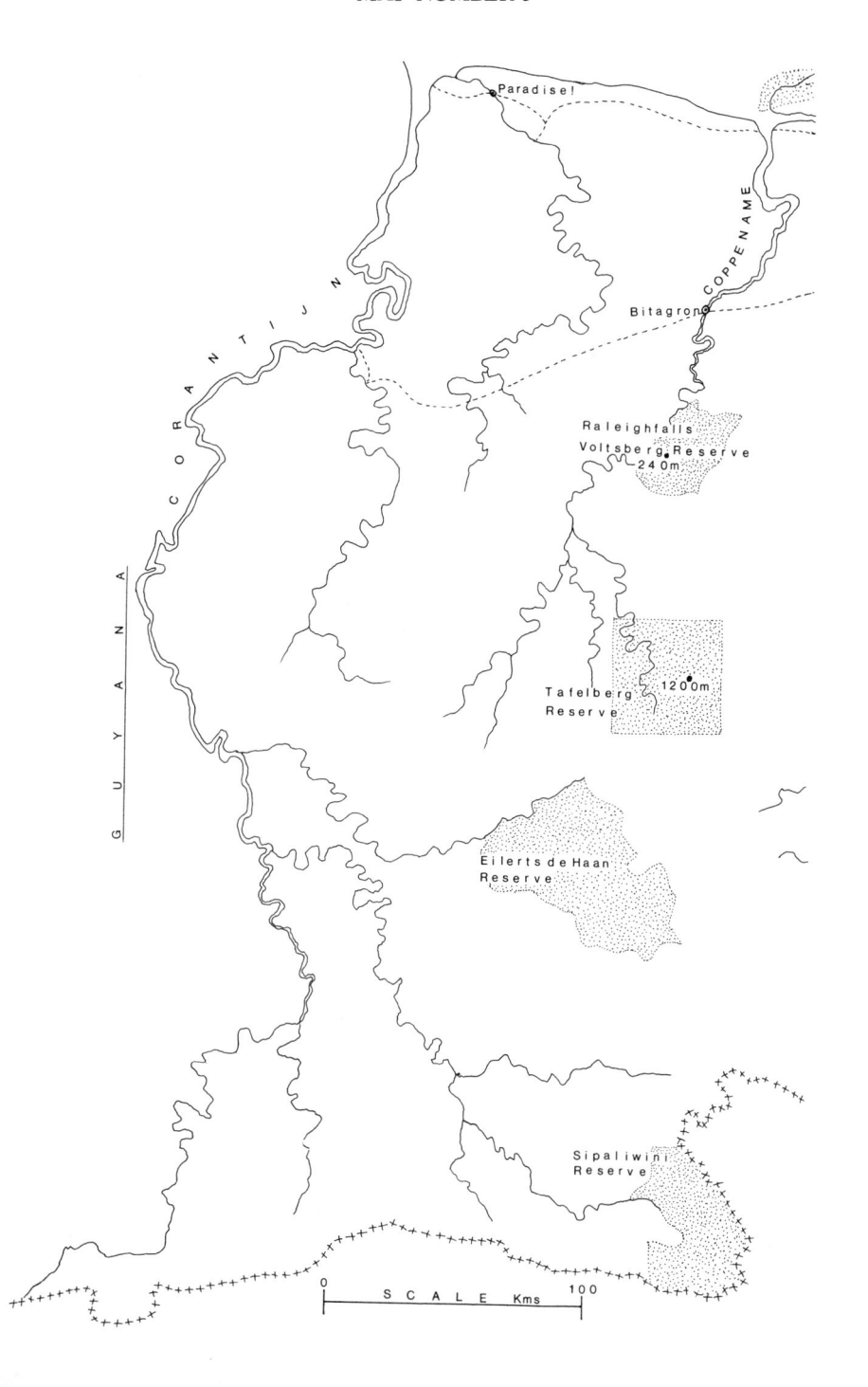

Maybe we should have taken this incident as a sign that this was going to be one of those days that are best spent safely indoors, but we didn't, and within the hour we set off upstream. The engine purred smoothly and we reckoned that the 50-km. journey would take us five or six hours. Eight hours of daylight were still left, which gave us a good safety margin. We were not equipped for camping out, as most of our gear, including tent and hammocks, had gone up to our destination ahead of us with some STINASU workers in a big dugout canoe.

Except for a couple of small villages tucked away in the jungle, there are no landmarks between Bitagron and the reserve. Raleigh Falls is a set of heavy rapids just above the camp and we reckoned that when we saw these we'd know that we'd arrived, even if we missed spotting the camp itself.

At about 3 P.M. things began to go wrong. Smoke poured from the outboard engine and it began producing odd, unhealthy sounds before losing power. The trouble wasn't serious but it took us two hours to put it right and by then there was little more than an hour of daylight left and we had no idea how far we still had to go.

It began to drizzle and the light failed prematurely beneath a leaden sky while we slid slowly through the water at half throttle, beginning to feel thoroughly fed up with this river trip. As darkness gathered it started to rain in earnest, the water falling so thick and heavy that it was difficult for us to keep our eyes open. Dom bailed with a plastic cup while I lay in the prow shining a flashlight onto the riverside bushes and Tanis drove us along, steering the boat parallel to the margin of the stream guided by the wavering yellow light. There's nowhere to shelter in a tropical storm; it's just as wet in the forest as it is in the open and as we had no tent, there was really no point in stopping.

Without warning the world was suddenly lit up by a flash of lightning so blindingly brilliant that for a second we saw river, sky, and jungle in glorious technicolor, and in the distance, towering above the trees, a dome-shaped mountain of gray rock that could only be Voltzberg. A deafening clap of thunder followed almost immediately and I dropped the flashlight (in the canoe, thank goodness), Tanis stalled the engine, and Dom mumbled something neither of us could understand. The flashlight was found, the engine restarted, and shakily we continued. We couldn't work out whether or not lightning would be likely to strike our canoe. The consensus was that it probably wouldn't. The next flash was more terrifying than the first and it helped us to reach a decision: We pulled into the bank and tied up to a bush. There was no shallow water to run the boat aground and the vegetation hung like a curtain right down to the water's surface, so we just sat there in the rain waiting for the storm to pass.

A cold, wet, miserable hour later the rain eased back to a mild drizzle. The electrical activity now seemed safely far off and we started up again, creeping slowly along the edge guided by the flashlight. Hours passed and we began to wonder if we'd still be going when the dawn arrived. The only food we'd thought to bring was a bag of fruit and the last piece had been eaten long ago.

Eventually, made reckless by discomfort and monotony we pulled out into midstream and got up some speed. The river was wide and deep and although we could see only a few meters into the inky night, I was confident that if I shone the light straight ahead I would see any obstacle in time to shout a warning to Tanis. I should have known better. As we skimmed along at full throttle, gaining confidence by the minute, a wall of impenetrable blackness loomed up before us and before I could even open my mouth we hit the jungle head-on and the canoe dived into the bushes with a sickening, scraping crash. We were right out of the water and, amazingly, none of us was injured. Just as we were wondering what to do next, Tanis saw a light shining through the tree. We'd arrived at the camp.

The Raleigh Falls rapids at Foengoe Island are 160 km. from the Atlantic Ocean and are the first cataracts you encounter traveling upstream. A few years ago, a whale swam up the Coppename River heading toward Raleigh Falls. Eventually the creature died and was washed up on a jungle bank to the mighty astonishment of the local people. This whale's skelton is now on display in Paramaribo's natural history museum.

The resistant rocks that produce the rapids demonstrate the nature of the country's interior, a rugged land of hills and mountains. Ten km. east of the rapids a 400-m.-high granite hill pokes up out of the steaming jungle. This is Voltzberg and we'd first seen it from the river during the thunderstorm. Voltzberg is an inselberg (island mountain) and there are scores of them scattered throughout the Surinam landscape, weathered remnants from another geological era.

We intended to spend three weeks living in the forest somewhere near the mountain, so we crossed the river to the mainland and, with loaded rucksacks, set off among the trees along a well-trodden path. It was the rainy season and the ground was muddy until we started to climb up away from the river. We heard peccaries nearby on three occasions but the only animals we saw on the trail were big red crabs that take to the high ground at this time of year.

That afternoon we made camp beside a stream and early the following morning walked up the steeply sloping face of Voltzberg. Clumps of bushes, cacti, and other water-conserving plants spring from crevasses in the rough gray surface, a flora quite distinct from the lush forest that surrounds it. The rock supports its own little ecosystem. From the summit the view is of hills, serpentine rivers, and endless green forest. Sounds of birds and animals were carried up to us with surprising clarity and we could see vividly hued birds in the treetops below.

There are snakes in the forest around Voltzberg. One day Tanis was clambering over a tree trunk when a long, thin, brown snake reared up right beside her. It made no attempt to strike but remained there, half its body vertical and motionless until long after she had fled. Another time we found an emerald tree boa draped over a low branch above a creek. I prodded it gently with a stick and it slowly unwound, slipped gracefully into the water with hardly a splash and glided away beneath the surface. It was fully 3 m. long and without doubt the most beautiful snake any of us had ever seen. A third colorful snake we came across was a king snake. Decorated with vividly contrasting bands of red, white, and black, it could easily have been mistaken for a venomous coral snake. In fact, the king snake is a much larger reptile and perfectly harmless.

Our most dramatic encounter with animals occurred on an afternoon when we were returning to camp through a grove of slender palms and saplings whose crowns formed a broken canopy only 2 m. above our heads. Without warning an alarmingly loud noise of crashing and breaking branches bore down on us from the left and within seconds, before we had time to become frightened, we were surrounded by monkeys, scrambling and swinging through the branches above us and to each side of us, some of them close enough to reach out and touch. They were small, long-haired monkeys called *sakis* and there were hundreds of them. For several minutes they didn't notice us as we stood watching them stream past, then suddenly we were spotted. General panic broke out and the forest echoed with cries of alarm, then there was complete silence, with not a monkey to be seen anywhere. We walked out of our sheltered hiding place among the palms into an open, sunlit glade and there we were greeted by the most astonishing sight. In the high trees around us from every visible branch furry faces peered down in fascination. We were right in the middle of the troupe and had neatly split their numbers in half, but their confusion was short-lived and they soon began to move off into the forest giving the area in which we stood a wide berth. Not all of them moved away however; fifty or sixty remained to stare down at us. One leaned out too far from its precarious perch and plunged head first 15 m. to the ground. We found it sitting rubbing its head; then it made for the nearest tree and scurried up the trunk like a squirrel, apparently uninjured.

One more piece of excitement came our way before we returned to Foengoe Island. It happened during a hike when we came to a spot where a huge, ancient tree had fallen, leaving a sizable hole in the jungle canopy where the morning sunshine came through. We climbed onto the tree trunk and were sitting there resting when Tanis pointed to a spot 20 m. away where a black jaguar sat, staring at us intently. We were too surprised to do anything but sit there staring back. After half a minute the cat stood, stretched, and then sauntered away glancing at us once over its shoulder before disappearing like a shadow among the trees. Not one of us had thought of taking a photograph.

Bigisanti Beach, Wia Wia Bank

The coast of Surinam provides a shifting landscape of mangrove swamps, mud banks, and glittering beaches of sand and shells. The shores are washed by a warm brown sea and coastal features such as sandbanks migrate westward at a rate of 1 km. a year with new ones forming in their wake. Apart from some Carib Indians, few people live on the coast. The roads and towns of the modern world are several kilometers inland, above the swamps, where the rivers contain fresh water and the ground can be cultivated. Con-

Turtle conservation work, Tanis gathering eggs from an endangered nest made below the high tide level, to be incubated artificially. Wia Wia, Surinam.

sequently, this sparsely populated region is nothing less than a wildlife paradise just waiting to be explored by anybody who cares to go there. And there's plenty for bird-watchers to see: spoonbills, flamingos, scarlet ibis, eagles, harriers, hawks, and others too numerous to mention.

We spent five weeks working at a STINASU nature reserve at Bigisanti ("big sand") Beach, on Wia Wia Bank, which is one of the most important nesting places in the world for several species of marine turtles, including the giant leatherbacks.

In daylight Bigisanti Beach presents an extraordinary spectacle. Half buried in the golden sands are hundreds of tree trunks brought down from the hinterlands by the rivers and washed up on the coast to be sculpted by water, wind, and sand — an endless gallery of strangely contorted shapes, some of them 30 m. long. When we were there, pink and purple objects lay on the wet sand that at first sight appeared to be partially inflated rubber balloons. On closer inspection they turned out to be floats of the notorious stinging coelenterate, the Portuguese man-of-war, that winds and tides had marooned on the shore to die. A sting from one of these relatives of the jellyfish (when it's alive in the sea) can result in an agonizing death for a human being. In an emergency urine can help to inactivate the venom.

Sharks inhabit the coastal waters. We once found the body of a 2-m.-long hammerhead shark on the beach, black and swollen in the morning sunshine. Just a few weeks before our arrival a fisherman had fallen from a small boat and been pulled out of the water almost immediately by his companions but not before a shark had neatly removed one of his legs just below the knee.

At regular intervals turtle tracks across the sand, looking as if tractors have driven right out of the ocean to the top of the beach where a green field of soft-leaved plants known as survival weed stretches away to the forest. Female turtles leave the ocean at night, usually at high tide, and crawl up the beach. Each excavates a hole in the sand, lays a hundred or more eggs, then fills the hole and returns to the sea. Weeks later the eggs hatch within minutes of each other and scores of baby turtles come scrambling out of the hole and hurry down to the sea like an army of jerky clockwork toys. They are very vulnerable when undertaking their 30-m. dash the ocean, and the first time we witnessed the event we saw the vultures before we saw the turtles, five fierce-eyed, bald-headed birds hopping around tearing up turtles with their great hooked bills and gobbling down the gory pieces. Gulls swooped down like dive-bombers and carried turtles away. Crabs with huge pincers ambushed turtles from behind pieces of driftwood and dragged them into holes in the sand. A huge eagle stood on the sidelines observing the grizzly scene like some regal potentate. Shouting at the vultures had little effect; they were bloated and belligerent and hissed at us. We drove them away with sticks, though even then they didn't take flight but bounded bad-temperedly out of range. The eagle stood up straight and fixed us with a wide-eyed stare as if challenging us to come too close. We saw about twenty turtles reach the sea out of perhaps four times that number that had started the journey. Once in the water, catfish and sharks would take care of many of the rest. Indeed, from that entire batch only two or three would survive the first year. It's a hard life for a young turtle.

When darkness falls the land cools rapidly and a breeze sets toward the ocean carrying with it scents and sounds from the jungle. Only stars light the sky and there is no glow on the horizon because there are no human settlements anywhere near. Millions of microscopic light-producing organisms rise to the ocean surface at night and the waters develop an eerie luminescence and waves collapse in showers of sparkling foam on the shore. Even the wet sand lights up with a trail of pale green brightness when you drag your feet through it.

A night walk along the sand is a magical experience. Find some fresh turtle tracks, follow them up the beach, and soon you are standing beside the animal who made them. This might be a 2-m.-long, 300-kg. leatherback turtle seemingly oblivious to your presence while she lays her eggs in the sand. Great glutinous tears drip from her eyes but she's not really crying; it's just the means by which she excretes excess salt.

Our hosts at Bigisanti Beach were three Carib Indians who work for STINASU for part of the year. These men are from coastal tribes that traditionally live on turtle products. The depth of their knowledge and understanding of the animals is truly astonishing. For instance, they can tell whether or not a turtle egg is fertile simply by picking it up. They're always right and when asked how they know, they say things like "this egg is no good, it doesn't feel right."

We all lived in a hut on the beach, one of a group of small buildings and storage sheds that comprise the biological research station. About 3 km. along the beach to the east is another building where casual visitors can stay for self-catering excursions, and that's it. Nothing else man-made distracts from the wildness of the place.

Our work consisted of traveling the length of Bigisanti on a motor bike each morning to identify and record the sites of nests made the previous night. It was pretty easy to tell which of five species of turtle had come ashore by the size of the tracks. The other job was to dig out the eggs from some sites made too near the water (the turtles don't always choose the best sites) and relocate them where they would be safe from high tides. Other batches of eggs we dug up and took back to the research station to be artificially incubated in styrofoam boxes.

When a box of eggs hatched we would carry it down to the wet sand and tip the tiny animals out in a writhing heap. After they had disentangled themselves a strange thing would happen; they would begin wandering off in random directions, some of them even heading back up the beach away from the ocean as if intent on returning to the research station. This behavior is in marked contrast to the animals that emerge from the natural nests in the beach; so intent are these individuals on making unerringly for the water that if an obstacle such as a stone is placed in their path they will try to climb over it rather than deviate from their route.

Anytime we were not working, we'd fish in the nearby tidal creek. When a large hook is baited with fish guts, tied to the end of a rope, and thrown into that creek at the turn of the tide, it is unusual to have to wait more than sixty seconds before pulling out a catfish of a size that will provide a substantial meal for three people. This outrageously easy pastime was an important commercial sideline for our friends. They cured the fish by splitting them open, sprinkling salt on the flesh, then laying them out on a rack over a smoky driftwood fire. A sheet of corrugated iron would be placed over the top and there they were left to "cook" for two days. When the men go on leave they take with them sacks full of the leathery, smoke-blackened, shriveled carcasses to sell in the market in Paramaribo. This activity is not discouraged by the foundation as it's not carried out on a scale that could cause ecological damage to the area.

Other fish besides catfish live in these creeks. In the shade of the bank lie shoals of so-called four-eyed fish, many of them right out of the water on the soft mud. These odd creatures have long, tapering bodies and huge bulbous eyes on top of their heads. If disturbed they sail out across the surface of the soupy water like flotillas of strange little boats. They're called four-eyed fish because the eyes are constructed with the upper part suitable for vision in the air and the lower part for vision underwater.

On two occasions we caught small sharks and their tender white meat made a delicious change from the bland and rather tough catfish. Another time we caught a fish with green, metallic-looking skin that lay on the ground curiously inert as if it didn't particularly mind being brought out of the water into the sunshine. One of our friends regarded this fish with undisguised horror and revulsion and gingerly pushed it back into the water with a stick explaining to us that it was deadly poisonous even to touch.

Animals come to Bigisanti Beach; deer browse on beach plants, small mammals feed on crabs, and occasionally jaguars come to kill and carry off the nesting turtles. The sandbanks are flanked by mangrove swamps, the land builders. Where the mangroves meet the sea, turbulent water loses its energy among the dense network of roots and deposits its muddy sediment. This is bound and stabilized by the plants and as new shoots take root in the newly made ground, decade by decade the green coastal belt moves outward into the sea. The coastal swamp forests can be visited via numerous tidal creeks and it's here that you can see the amazing diversity of the local bird life, including rookeries of scarlet ibis.

It was in this region that the first European settlers made their homes, a little distance inland on the old coastal plain. From all accounts these Dutch settlers had a pretty tough time of it, dying like flies from a variety of diseases, constantly at war with Indians, escaped slaves, and the British and other Europeans, and they eventually gave up and deserted their swampy home for new pastures. Some of the wooden buildings of the old towns and villages still stand, ghostly and forgotten among the huge trees and still black waters. Special permission from the foundation is required to visit these sites, but it's well worth the trouble of arranging a trip. With an early morning mist hanging over the scene the atmosphere is delightfully creepy and mysterious.

One impression that's difficult to avoid is that those early Dutch settlers must have spent most of their time manufacturing glass bottles and jars. It seems as though every household in Paramaribo has a collection of these artifacts, and bottles of all shapes, sizes, and colors are on sale in the shops and on the streets. Glassware is being found constantly; you can see workmen engaged in ditch-digging and canal clearance carefully sifting through the dirt for old bottles. During our stay at Wia Wia we found four irregularly shaped, seamless, blown-glass bottles washed up by the tide. For all we knew they could have been of sufficient historical interest to make museum exhibits.

In case you do plan to visit a coastal reserve, it would be unfair of us not to mention a few minor discomforts and inconveniences. Biting insects can be a real nuisance; remember to pack the insect repellant. It can become unbearably hot and although you could take a dip in the ocean, the water contains sharks, Portuguese men-of-war, and God knows what else. The supply of fresh water is collected in tanks from the rain that falls on the roofs of the buildings and is far too precious to permit you to shower whenever you feel like it. But if our description of the delights these areas have to offer excites you, then the discomforts will be of no significance.

Jaguar
Of the world's felines, only tigers and lions exceed jaguars in size. Jaguars have the distinction of being the only cats that kill their prey by biting through the skull, and can do this to a fully grown cow! Jaguars are shy of man, don't attack unless provoked, and are never man-eaters. The greatest danger jaguars face is being hunted for their pelts.

The Bush Negroes Of Surinam

Beside the rivers of Surinam's undeveloped interior live tribes of pure-blood West African people. They are the descendents of escaped slaves who parted company with their British and Dutch masters in the seventeenth century and established themselves in the South American jungle with such success that they were able to wage war on their former persecutors, and at one stage almost succeeded in driving the European colonists from that part of South America.

Slaves were first brought to the colony of Surinam by the British, then in 1674 Surinam was traded to Holland in exchange for what is now New York. It was prior to the time when the country came under Dutch control that the Bush Negroes developed their language. It's called Taki-Taki and is derived from the Elizabethan English of William Shakespeare's day.

Unlike their indigenous Amerindian neighbors, the Bush Negroes are a river rather than a forest people, and their skill at navigating the dangerous rocky waters of Surinam's hinterland in long heavy dugout canoes cannot be excelled by anybody on that continent.

These several thousand proud and fiercely independent black people live in numerous small villages and follow an ancient, traditional tribal life transported from the jungles of West Africa and replanted in the jungles of South America, complete with West African art, drums, dances and spirit and ancestor worship. The only sad note is that increasingly the young men are leaving the jungle villages, donning western clothes, and going to work and live in and around the city.

In most literature on this subject, Bush Negroes are referred to as Djukas. I guess people find the latter name more acceptable than the former, but it's incorrect. The Djukas are only one of several tribes of Bush Negroes, and the people involved refer to themselves (and always have done) as Bush Negroes.

Caution: Bush Negroes are friendly, well-mannered people but they don't take kindly to insensitive tourists who wander around villages snapping pictures of everybody and everything as if they were visiting a zoo.

Bush Negro Village Scene
The men build houses, carve out canoes, hunt, and fish. The women seem to do just about everything else. In this scene the woman in the foreground is pounding corn. On the hut are typically stylized symbolic designs executed by, and unique to, one family. In the background a sacred shrine stands beneath a "biggy-bong."

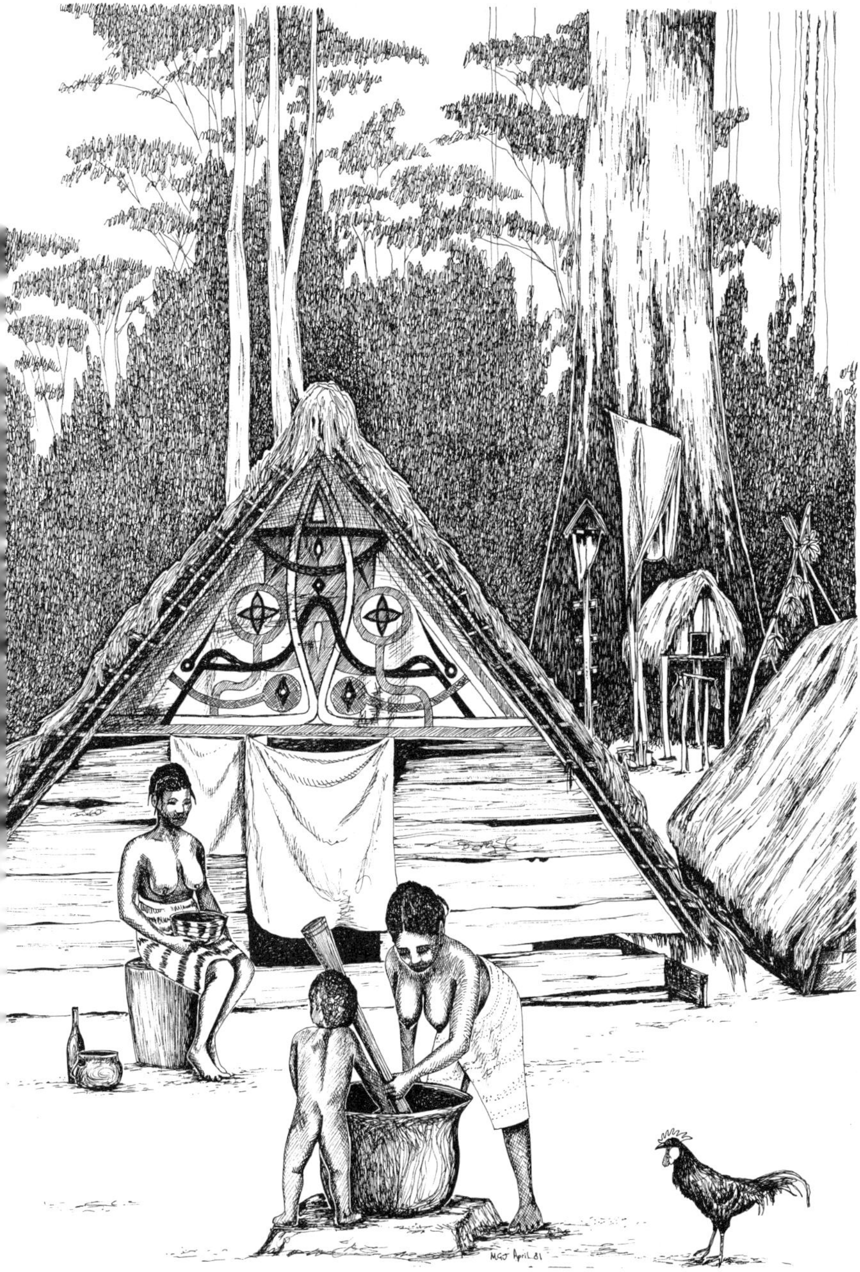

The Tapanahoni River

The most convenient place in the interior of Surinam to set off on an expedition from is an island on the Marowijne (pronounced marror wine) River called Stoelmanseiland. It has a large hospital serving the needs of the local Bush Negro people, a government guest house (expensive), a police station, a military camp, a couple of Bush Negro villages, and two shops where you can buy food, beer, some clothing, hardware, machetes, and other supplies. There is a landing strip and regular flights serve the island. You can also get there by canoe from Albina, which can be easily reached by bus from Paramaribo. By canoe it's a one-day journey up some exciting rapids. Go to the waterfront at Albina and ask around; there's plenty of river traffic carrying supplies and you should get a cheap ride. You can try to haggle over the price but the boatmen are usually pretty fair.

From Stoelmanseiland you can travel upstream onto the Tapanahoni or Lawa rivers. There's not much regular traffic on these rivers and it becomes scarcer the higher you go, but of course things also get more interesting, wild, and picturesque: Go far enough on either river and you'll be in unexplored country. To hire a boat and crew to take you from Stoelmanseiland to the far south of the country would be very expensive and is a long, and, in places, dangerous, journey.

Our Tapanahoni River trip was the result of a happy accident. This was our first visit to a tropical country and we took a regular airplane flight from Paramaribo to Stoelmanseiland with the idea of spending a week seeing a bit of that notorious South American jungle. At Stoelmanseiland we were befriended by a group of Surinamese who were working on a malaria eradication program and were preparing to go far upriver to remote Bush Negro villages to spray huts with insecticides, distribute medicated salt, and take blood samples from the populace for later laboratory analysis. The outcome of this chance meeting was that we were invited to accompany them and we spent the next few months traveling the rivers.

Our craft was a 10-m.-long dugout canoe powered by a 40-h.p. outboard engine. The Tapanahoni River has numerous sets of rapids; to get up these the motorist had the assistance of two men in the prow armed with long poles to push the canoe away from rocks and prevent its swinging sideways into the current. The scenery was lovely, the riverside jungle broken only by an occasional little clearing where people stood and waved to us. Fish jumped in the wide, deep river as we slid by, and on the foaming rapids the exposed rocks were covered with plants in purple flower.

In the early afternoon of the first day upriver from Stoelmanseiland, we stopped at a Bush Negro village. It consisted of a clearing in which stood rows of board and palm-thatch dwellings surrounded by high green forest. A huge jungle tree, spared from the axe, had been left towering over the center of the clearing. The people call this tree a *biggy bong* and it was accorded magical significance. Beneath it were a shrine and a bizarre assortment of religious artifacts: upside-down rum bottles half buried in the soil, sheets on poles, cooking pots hanging from strings. Interested to see what was contained within a tiny thatched hut, I opened the door to find a decomposing human corpse — I shut the door again quickly!

That night we slung our hammocks inside the largest building in the village, a huge barnlike place with a steeply sloping thatched roof, beautifully carved wooden door, and convenient gaps between the wall boards that permitted twenty or thirty inquisitive children to stand outside and watch us get ready for bed. The building was a "safe hut"; any man, woman, or child suffering violence at the hands of another could retreat to this hut until the elders were called and the case was heard and judged. The person rash enough to pursue the victim and perpetuate violence within the hut would be beaten, have his possessions confiscated, and then banished from the village forever. We were told that the building was seldom used for its protective purpose and then usually by women escaping from jealous men. The village elders are presided over by the village chief, called a captain, and his right-hand man or woman called a *basha*. Above the captain is a granman or king who visits the villages of his people from time to time.

On the next morning we made our first excursion into the jungle accompanied by a young man named Anapai. Anapai wanted to take us hunting and he borrowed an ancient shotgun from the captain for this purpose. The gun had a long barrel, no stock, and the cartridges were too large for the bore and had to be forced into position with a stick. We decided that if at any time during our excursion Anapai looked like pressing the trigger of that lethal weapon, we'd cover our heads and throw ourselves on the jungle floor.

We set off at a surprisingly rapid pace along a trail that was all but invisible to us, weaving back and forth through a world of dappled sunlight and tall trees with trunks as straight as stone columns, their crowns lost in the leafy ceiling high overhead. After half an hour we sat down on a log for a much-needed rest. Not a single monkey, snake, or jaguar had we seen; in fact, the only animal we had noticed was a small brown moth and we were both a bit disappointed. True, there were many strange noises, but otherwise this jungle seemed to us a pretty lifeless place. Then Anapai pointed at the ground and there in the earth were two large paw prints: Even we could see that they'd been made quite recently by a large heavy cat and although the animal was nowhere in sight, the jungle seemed suddenly more like the jungles we'd read about.

On we walked deeper into the forest till we came to a swampy area and Anapai carefully picked his way around a clump of harmless-looking, waist-high grass. Tanis and I simply blundered through the middle of it and emerged on the other side with our arms and legs covered with blood. We'd discovered razor grass! The cuts were very shallow and would heal rapidly but there were dozens of them and they stung for quite a while.

Scattered around the base of a thorny palm tree we found some brown, hard-shelled nuts. Anapai cracked one open with his machete blade, removed a white object from inside, bit it in half, and gave me the other half. It was soft and tasted sweet and creamy. "That was a grub you just ate," observed Tanis and indeed it was. Anapai was busy cracking open the nuts and removing the round, fat grubs from inside.

Later that morning Anapai stopped still, looked around, then turned to us and said "we loss mister," which left us in no doubt that we were indeed lost. I'd read that being lost in the jungle was nearly as serious as being lost in the desert or at sea. Now the big trees and knotty vines, the strange hoots and howls all seemed frightening and hostile. We walked along behind Anapai losing confidence in him by the minute.

Four hours later, hot, tired, and hungry, Anapai rediscovered the trail. He was happy again, so were we, and the jungle was a friendly, fascinating place as we headed back to the village talking and joking, pointing out the butterflies and birds. Anapai told us about an uncle of his who went out hunting and became lost. "What happened to him?" I asked. Anapai shrugged his shoulders and smiled politely. "Do you mean he never came back?" asked Tanis. Anapai nodded. "Him loss, him never come back."

In the weeks that followed, we continued upriver stopping at village after village sometimes for a couple of hours, sometimes for several days. The further we traveled the less evidence there was of the modern world until one day we walked into a place where a group of women watched in open-mouthed wonder as we waded ashore from the canoe. One of them even dropped in the river the bundle she had been holding. "They never see white man before," one of our hosts explained casually. These folk knew of white people and most of the men had met one or two, but the women and children who had never been far beyond their village had never seen the likes of us before. When they'd overcome their initial surprise, we were besieged by hoardes of children who vigorously rubbed our skin to see if it was painted and pulled Tanis' long blonde hair to see if it would come off and tried to pull down my pants, presumably to determine what kind of genitalia I possessed. We were a big hit with the village folk that day.

The captain was a friendly old man who took an immediate liking to us. Tanis and I sat one either side of him on little wooden stools encircled by the fifty or sixty villagers, while our friends from the AMC told him what they wanted to do, namely, take blood samples from the people (the tip of the finger is pricked and a spot of blood put onto a microscope slide). The captain came to a decision and pointed first at me, then at a woman standing in the crowd. Unexpectedly she gave a cry, turned around, and fled, knocking over two children in her panic. A crowd of jubilant women pursued her through the village. While she was being dragged back toward us, kicking, shouting, and struggling, the situation was explained to us. This woman was one of the captain's wives and she'd been chosen by him to donate a blood sample. Furthermore, I had been selected to perform the operation. Four women sat on the victim while another two forcibly unclenched her fist. I pricked the finger, blood flowed, everybody cheered and clapped, the captain slapped me on the back and then went to fetch a bottle of rum to celebrate my demonstration of surgical skill.

During our travels on the Tapanahoni we met one granman, a tribal chief of some twenty villages. He was in residence on a steep-sided island and the first hint we had that somebody important lived there was the sight of a dead vulture strung from a branch over the water and positioned so that any boat coming into the landing bay had to pass beneath it. Clearly there was some special kind of magic associated with this place. At the end of a neat row of ordinary huts was a larger wooden building with elaborate wood carvings — the granman's dwelling. We were escorted to "the presence" by a wizened old man in a loincloth who instructed us as to how we should behave while we stayed in this place. He told us solemnly that "When you are near the granman's house you should not run, shout, fire your gun, or shit."

The granman was a surprisingly young, friendly man who gave us the impression that he'd just been waiting for someone to come and visit so that he could open a bottle of rum. It was only 8 A.M. and we'd had no breakfast, but we'd become accustomed to the early morning drinking sessions. It seems to be the favorite time for Bush Negroes to drink. The procedure goes like this. The host (in this case the granman) opens the bottle and chants a prayer, all the while splashing rum onto the ground as an offering. (I've seen half the bottle go at this stage during an outburst of religious fervor while the guests look on anxiously, no doubt praying that the host doesn't get so carried away as to tip the whole lot out!) After this, rum is poured into a cup and handed to the first guest who swallows the contents in one gulp and hands it back. It's refilled and passed to the next guest and so on. If you're not in the habit of swallowing half a cupful of neat, white rum before breakfast, the experience adds a whole new dimension to drinking.

Our day with the granman developed into quite a party. While we could all still walk we made it outside into the fresh air and the men got out the drums: huge, barrel-shaped constructions, some of them over a meter high. First the children danced and then the men. Some of the dancers became frenzied and threw themselves onto the ground as if in convulsions, while others danced down to the river and leapt into the water. Later the women danced and this was a positively sedate affair by comparison; they shuffled around in a big circle while the men drummed, sang, and clapped. The celebrations continued all day and on into the evening and that night, with the big drums booming out over the forest, I dreamed that I was one of those nineteenth century explorers of deepest Africa. I didn't feel as if I'd spent that day in South America at all.

Eventually we arrived at the very edge of Bush Negro country. Beyond us to the south were a few Indian settlements and beyond that lay unexplored country of small rocky rivers, hills, and mountains. Here we met up with two canoes of Trios Indian braves, who had come down to trade with the Bush Negroes. They carried hunting dogs (mostly small puppies), piles of jungle fruits, and bundles of vines. These Indians wore only loincloths and some had red stains on their skins. Many wore strands of red and blue beads round their necks, wrists, and ankles. There were no outboard engines on the canoes; they were propelled by wooden paddles. Nor were guns and knives to be seen, only bows and long, wood-tipped arrows. Indeed there was nothing about this group to suggest that the twentieth century had arrived.

Our final excursion was to a sacred mountain called Teboe Top, a place of pilgrimage for both Bush Negroes and Indians. We were told that although we would be able to see the mountain from the river, we mustn't stare at it or mention it or else it would disappear; we had to behave as though it did not exist until we actually set foot on it. Also, we had to climb it barefoot.

Eight of us made the journey: two Indians, four of our crew, and ourselves. The sacred mountain came dramatically into view, a dome-shaped granite hill swathed in mist, only about 300 m. high but an impressive sight nevertheless, not least because it looked so incongruously bare sticking up out of that rich jungle.

It seemed ludicrous to ignore such a conspicuous object, but we all stuck to the rules and gazed solemnly at the river ahead. The canoe was beached at a well-trodden spot where a tell-tale gap in the greenery showed a jungle trail, and off we went, the two Indians in red loincloths carrying bows and arrows in the lead. We climbed through dense forest for a while and then we emerged into the sunshine at the foot of the mountain. From here it really did look enormous and very steep. We took off our shoes and began the ascent; soon we were on all fours to get over the worst parts. Prickly bramble-like plants grew in patches over the rocky surface and here and there were clumps of bushes, but otherwise the rock was bare. When we were about halfway up we came to a Bush Negro shrine with the usual tattered white sheet on a propped-up pole like some ghostly scarecrow. Beneath it, along with numerous gifts of bottled beer and wood carvings, were coins and bank notes, some of them of high value, weighted down with stones. Not one of our companions gave these items as much as a second glance.

The view from the summit was splendid. Stretching to the horizon in every direction was unbroken forest with scores of "mountains," many of them similar to the one on which we sat. Much of what we could see must have been very remote country. One of the crew told us a story about two children who had climbed the mountain and found a cave. They went inside and the mouth of the cave closed up. The mountain had swallowed them. Sometimes, he told us, you could hear them knocking to get out. I found myself listening to hear it.

NEED A MAP?

Bradt Enterprises imports topographical maps from Latin America. If we don't have the maps you want in stock, we'll be happy to order them for you.

We also have city maps and road maps of many South and Central American countries.

Why not send for a catalog?

Survival International (SI), a registered charity in Britain with no religious or political affiliations, was founded in London in 1969 to promote the welfare of tribal peoples worldwide. The organization serves as consultant to the UN and the EEC, and national chapters have been formed in the USA and other countries.

Survival International has three main objectives:
1. To help tribal peoples to exercise their rights to survival and self-determination.
2. To ensure that the interests of tribal peoples are properly represented in all decisions affecting their future.
3. To secure the ownership and use of land and resources by tribal peoples.

To further these objectives, SI supports projects with tribal peoples, advocates on their behalf on an international level, and publishes materials on their predicament. SI focuses particularly on the urgent situation of South American Indians.

To support South American Indians in their struggle for survival, contact: The International Secretariat
Survival International
36 Craven Street
London WC2N 5NG
England

Giant Anteater
A beautiful and inoffensive creature, the giant anteater is capable of defending itself with incredible ferocity, using the powerful claws of the front feet. There is a recorded instance of a giant anteater killing a fully grown jaguar in a battle.

Taki-Taki

The fact that Taki-Taki is a pidgin dialect derived largely from English is not obvious until one has become accustomed to the sound and hence able to appreciate the structure of the sentences. For example:
I have a headache
How much does it cost
I have a cough

mi éde áti mi
ó men mi mu pai
mi néki méki kookoo

(literally: my head hurt me)
(literally: how many me must pay)
(literally: my neck make kookoo)

Not all sentences are as obvious as these three examples. Acute accents indicate stress in speaking.

The language is spoken quickly and nasally, and in a sing-song way that's rather hypnotic. Verbs have no tenses, nouns have no plurals nor genders. These and other aspects make Taki a fairly easy language for an English-speaking person to learn. In fact, once you know the rules you can pretty well make it up as you go along, though this is not to suggest that Taki is in any way an inferior tongue. It's merely flexible and adaptable.

Taki-Taki (not Dutch) is the language used by the vast majority of Surinamese people. It varies from place to place around the country. For instance, in Saramacca District Saramacca tongo *is spoken, which contains some Portuguese. The Taki-Taki spoken in the towns differs in only minor ways from the language spoken by the Bush Negroes of the interior.*

NOTE: *Some of the Bush Negro people have a second African language that is not used with outsiders. We know of no English/Taki-Taki dictionary, phrase book, or teach-yourself publication.*

The following is in part a phrase and word guide but more importantly a learning aid. With this list committed to memory, you will be well on the way to an understanding of Taki. Accents emphasize the syllables. Pronunciation:

"o" as in "dot"
"i" as in "lid"
"e" as in "bed"
"a" as the u in "hut"

Does anyone here understand English?	sáma a de ya di sábi ínglisi no?
I don't understand Taki.	mi no sábi táki
Whom should I ask?	sámi mi moo ákisi?
Where (is)?	on pe?
How far?	on lánga?
Can we bathe?	oo sa go wási no?
You must not swim there.	oo no moo can swen da pe
Will you show me where it is?	kon go soi mi pe a de?
I (don't) think so.	mi (a) dénki so
This is my wife/friend.	dísi a mi oomang/máti
I'm here on vacation/work.	mi kon nyáng fakánsi/wróko
I'm in a hurry.	mi moo de hési hési
I'm ready.	mi kába
Go, walk, drive, paddle slowly, quietly, gently.	wáka sáfi sáfi
I want to go to the city.	mi wáni go a foto
I am hungry.	ángi moo mi
bite, eat or food	nyáng
catch fish	kísi físi
banana	bakúba
yesterday	ésde
doctor	dáta
white person	báka
upriver	tápoo na líba
a boatman	wan bótoman
waterfall, rapids	soela

Wayana Men Preparing Canes for Arrows
Canes for arrow shafts are made from the stem of a reed. Dried, a 1-m. length weighs only 15g.

The Wayana Indians Of Southeast Surinam

As members of a general fact-finding expedition, we traveled into Wayana territory and lived among the people for six weeks. The Upper Marowijne (also called the Lawa River) is a beautiful river. Stones are its most distinctive feature: Great, rounded boulders resembling giant tortoises emerge from the surface when the water level drops in the dry season. The stones provide a clue to the nature of the country through which the river flows. It is a rocky, picturesque landscape of hills and mountains covered with that seemingly endless carpet of tropical rain forest.

In places our motorist had difficulty finding a passage through gravelly shallows and we frequently had to get out and wade along beside the canoe. On the rapids it took all eleven of us to haul it across the rocks. The dugout was 15 m. long and we still had two 50-gallon drums of gas left, which added to the weight.

Half a day after leaving the remotest Bush Negro village we were in Indian country and soon arrived at a sizable riverside clearing in which stood rows of large, conical, palm-thatched huts. The first impression we received on entering this Wayana village was of redness. The men wore loincloths made of bright red material and the women wore the same vivid cloth either as a simple wrap-around skirt or as a frontal flap suspended from a cord around the waist. Many of the women had their arms and legs stained red with vegetable dye. Some of the men had clusters of red feathers pushed through their earlobes. At the edge of the clearing stood a row of six bamboo cages on poles 1 m. above the ground. These contained lean, snarling, mad-eyed, salivating hunting dogs and for some reason that we were never able to discover, these ferocious animals were also stained red. (Twice daily a dog's owner takes it to the river, washes it, and recolors its fur.) We were greeted by a small, naked, copper-skinned child who gave each of us a banana. The banana skins were deep red!

We were seated on benches in a long hut with the men of the village. In order to show them what a friendly fellow I was, I offered the man sitting next to me my tobacco so that he could roll himself a cigarette. He indicated that he would accept one but that I should make it for him, which I did. The man next to him then waved at me to convey the message that he would like a cigarette, too. Finally when I'd rolled cigarettes for every one of the fourteen men in the group and was just about to put away the tin, the first man informed me that he had now finished his cigarette and was ready for another one! I could see no end to this farcical situation and wondered how long our precious supply of tobacco would last at this rate.

Although the Wayanas accept whatever is offered and ask for anything they like the look of, they give what they have just as readily. In the evenings we would wander through the village among little groups of people sitting around wood fires cooking and eating. Invariably we would be offered food, which was usually a kind of stew with fish and starchy vegetables and side dishes of fruit and turtles eggs. Sometimes there would be roasts of game hunted in the forest, many kinds of monkey, tapir, deer, various rodents, land tortoises, lizards, and even parrots and toucans. (The Wayana won't eat the male spider monkey, though, as they believe that once long ago a Wayana brave turned into a spider monkey and to kill one might mean killing a relative.) For a while we felt guilty about eating the local wildlife, but rationalized our feelings with the thought that the animals were not being killed for our benifit; the meat was simply there for us to try if we wished to do so.

One afternoon a hunter came in from the forest with a red howler monkey he'd shot with an arrow and we watched him prepare it for the pot. First it was dipped into boiling water and then the fur was carefully scraped off with a knife, leaving the skin intact. The skin was pinkish white and when the defurred animal was held up it looked so shockingly like a human child that several of our party could not bring themselves to eat any part of it when it was cooked.

The main center of Wayana population is a big village called Anapaike. Here a family of mission members live in a wooden house near a landing strip used by mission airplanes. The man in charge told us about recent contacts made with the Akuriyo Indians, a primitive Carib-speaking hunter/gatherer people who wander through the forests of southeast Surinam and neighboring Brazil. They live in small groups and keep to the creeks and deep forest away from the main rivers. They cannot make fire and the women carry it with them, never allowing it to die out and rekindling it at regular intervals. In the early 1970s many Akuriyos were contacted and went to live in Trios Indian villages, but within two years 25 percent of them had died from such causes as chicken pox, dysentery, and psychological problems associated with adjustment. No doubt groups of uncontacted Indians still live in the vast and unexplored forest of southern Surinam. There is no shortage of stories about lost tribes. The records of Akuriyo life make fascinating reading. (See the bibliography: *The Akariyo of Surinam*.)

We left Anapaike and journeyed to a smaller village upstream where there were no missionaries. Here we were welcomed with a great show of enthusiasm and an hour after our arrival food was prepared for us and we were shown to a large shelter where a group of men sat on small stools around a low table of bound bamboo poles. The meal looked delicious: There were huge, flat, round pancakes of freshly baked cassava bread (bland, rather tough, and tasteless but very filling), piles of little turtle eggs still steaming from the boiling water, a selection of wild fruits, vegetables gathered from the forest, and several big chunks of cold, smoke-blackened meat and fish. Beside us was placed a great vat of cassiri, an alcoholic beverage made from cassava. I helped myself to the food and began chewing on a lump of meat. It was rather tough and a bit gamy for my liking, but I was enjoying it just the same. Tanis had selected something that looked like a tomato and she was eying it suspiciously. She loves tomatoes but one of the instructions from our old jungle survival handbook had become permanently imprinted on her mind. It said: "Never eat any wild fruit that resembles a tomato."

"Why don't you have some of this meat?" I asked her.

"No thanks," she replied. "It's crawling with maggots."

And it was, too; small white maggots were all over the piece I was holding, desperately wriggling away from the light as I rotated it in my hand. I turned my head politely away from the company and spat a mouthful of the half chewed meat on the ground. My fellow diners were not so fastidious. They were methodically picking the maggots from the meat and popping them into their mouths as if they were chocolate drops.

Cassiri is widely manufactured by the South American indians. In this village they produced this stuff in vast quantities; we saw half a canoe full of it in one place. It is made by fermenting cassava and small quantities of other ingredients such as bananas and pineapples. To add more potency the women chew up the ingredients and spit them into the must. After the meal a dozen of us sat in a circle around the vat full of fluid. A small, halved calabash of a half liter capacity was dipped into the brew and we drank from it in turns. The cassiri was milky looking and tasted a bit like diluted beer without the bitterness. It was quite pleasant but not very exciting.

After a couple of hours I estimated that I had consumed three or more liters of cassiri but apart from feeling uncomfortably bloated, nothing else was happening to me. I experienced no sense of intoxication and I doubted if the drink had even a quarter of the alcohol content of mild canned beer. In contrast to our condition the Indians were evidently becoming drunk. At regular intervals they left the group and went to a bush to urinate and were noticeably unsteady on their feet. One of the men was telling a story in a loud voice and everyone listened with rapt attention. Suddenly he stopped and was silent: He grasped his nose between thumb and forefinger and turning his head to one side, vomited. It came out like a jet of water from a hose and continued for several seconds. Then he wiped his mouth on the back of his hand and carried on with the story as if nothing had happened. Later, as the group became more drunken, several of the others did exactly the same thing.

These drinking session were a frequent occurrence but I never saw any antisocial behavior result from them. Everybody remained in good humor and the children used to gather round the drunken men and make fun of them without provoking anger.

The Wayana way of life seemed to us to be entirely without routine. People would lie in their hammocks all day and then quite unexpectedly become very active, taking up their bows and arrows to go on hunting or fishing expeditions, sometimes for days at a time. During our stay we developed the impression that they lived an enviable life of plenty, the forest full of game, rivers full of fish, and trees loaded with fruit. Indeed, huge yellow papayas fell to the ground and rotted where they lay because the Indians didn't particularly like this fruit. However, our impression was not objective. We were there in the middle of the dry season when the living is easy; for much of the year the living is correspondingly hard with swollen rivers, fishing and hunting extremely difficult, and little plant food available.

Missionaries and Indians

Many people dislike the idea of religious missionaries "civilizing" primitive tribes with the resulting loss of culture and tradition. Nevertheless, it has to be admitted that the religiously motivated are often the only ones willing to help Indians in deed as well as word, and South American Indians certainly need friends. Comparatively few anthropologists are prepared to devote their lives to the welfare of a small group of jungle Indians, whereas a great many missionaries do exactly that.

On the Upper Marowijne live Wayana Indians, a people who first experienced the regulating influence of the outside world more than a decade ago in the form of Christian missionaries who have lived and worked among them ever since. The mission has a strong influence over the Wayanas, though when we were there we felt that many groups were not too happy about the situation.

Whether or not a break away from modern Western man and his Christianity would be in the best interest of the Wayanas is open to debate. In the past they traded with, and were exploited by, the more wordly-wise Bush Negroes from downriver. The exploitation has been stopped by the missionaries. The Wayanas used to practice infanticide and the tribe's numbers became low with an unhealthy excess of males. The mission put a stop to this and they also strongly discouraged the import of liquor into the villages by traders from downriver. No objective observer could deny that this latter policy is thoroughly desirable because the Indians simply cannot handle strong drink. I don't know why this should be so; maybe there are physiological reasons for it. It's our observation that with their own home brew of mildly alcoholic cassiri they become happily intoxicated. With imported bottled beer they are far more excitable and sometimes violent. With rum, all inhibitions vanish and they become totally unpredictable. In the past murders have followed rum drinking sessions.

Three-Toed Sloth and Young
Because the sloth moves so slowly, its fur (which is often green with algae) provides a safe mobile home for a sedentary specis of moth.

Foods of Surinam

Paramaribo has an excellent, large, covered market encircled by eating booths. It opens early (6 A.M.) and closes at midday. Street stalls sell cooked noodles, rice, and chicken. These are cheap but sold out by mid-afternoon; they also sell beef satay, skewered beef in peanut sauce accompanied by chili sauce (hot and optional). Shops and cafés make sandwiches. The choice of fillings varies from shop to shop but the usual offerings are fat pork, curried egg prawns in sauce, fried eggs, beans in sauce, green beans and tomato, sliced cheese, and peanut butter (very popular in Surinam) all on show in bowls and scooped lavishly into fresh crusty long rolls. Again, these are usually sold out by noon. All shops are closed between noon and 3 P.M. Local foods include heaping plates of rice or noodles topped with chopped vegetables and small pieces of chicken seasoned with a delicious sauce. These are sometimes served with mixa meti *(mixed meats) instead of chicken. The dish is known as* nasi goreng *(rice) or* bhami goreng *(noodles). The beer, Parbo, is good, solid in liter bottles, and drunk very cold everywhere, anytime. Rijsttafel, rice table, is served at Indonesian restaurants. It consists of a selection of dishes served with rice at a round table. Try to go in a group; it's cheaper.*

MAP NUMBER 4

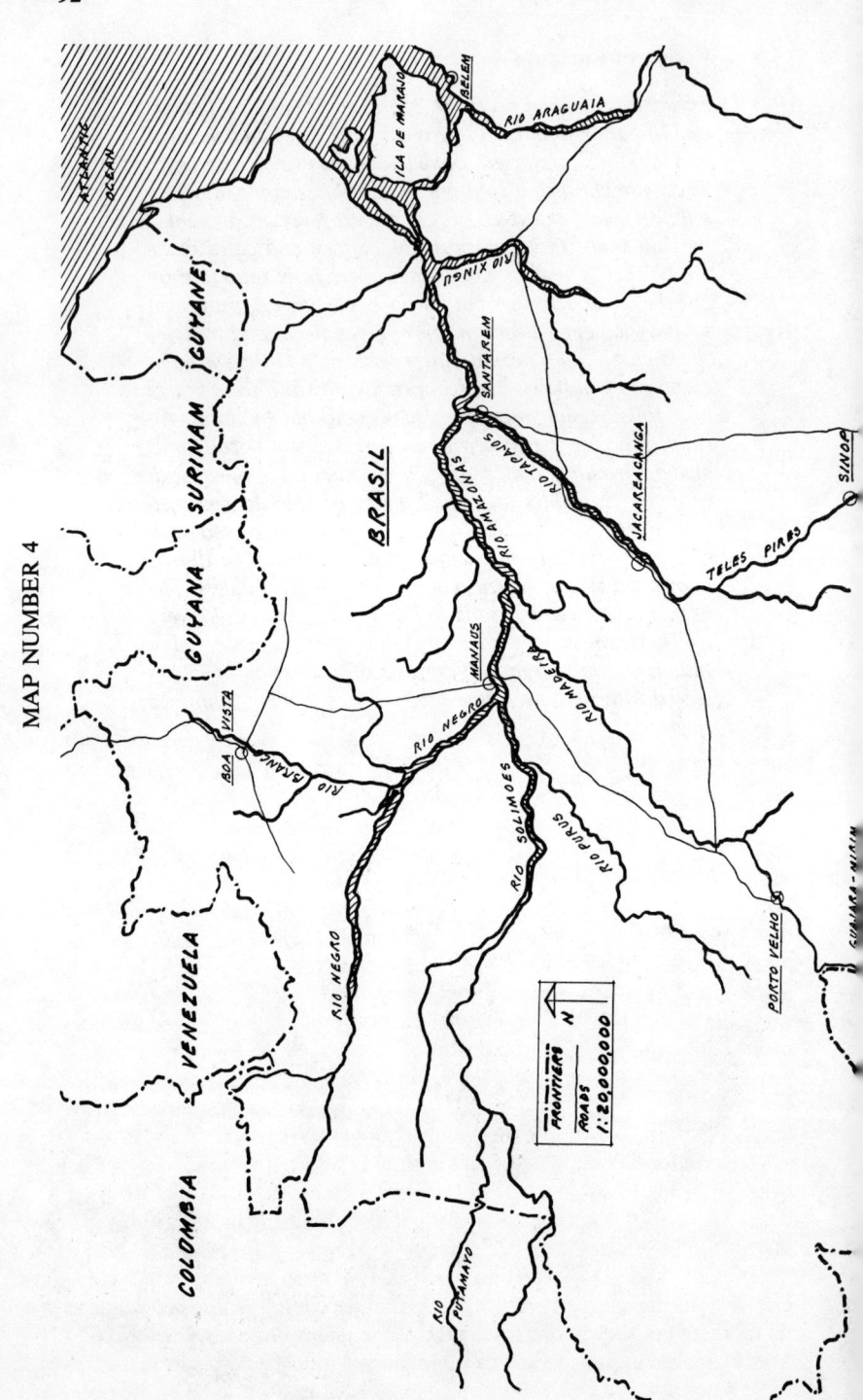

Canoeing in Brazilian Amazonia

By John Harrison

The idea to do our first canoe trip in Brazil came to Patricio (a Chilean) and myself (a Briton) at about 5 A.M. in a sleazy hotel in Boa Vista, north of Manaus. Brazilians shouldn't be allowed cassette recorders or radios in their possession before 9 A.M., because while others need coffee or a shower to face the day, Brazilians need only a dose of loud Samba. Already the hotel reverberated to three or four different tunes, cocks crowing babies' screams and disagreeable noises from the bathroom next door.

Anyway there we lay, scratching our new mosquito bites and discussing the horrific prospect of having to spend at least another week in Boa Vista because the road to Manaus was closed — one of the river ferries had sunk. The tourist attractions of Boa Vista can be guaged from the fact that by 6 A.M. we had decided to paddle 1,300 kms. down the rivers Branco and Negro to Manaus rather than stay here another week. By 3 P.M. we had bought a second-hand canoe that leaked alarmingly (50 dollars) hammocks, 5 kilos of rice, 2 kilos of beans, salt, fishing tackle, coffee, sugar, matches and 5 litres of rum. Neither of us had paddled a dugout before (nor anything else for that matter), and with our weight it sat alarmingly low in the water. However we put on an assured air as we wobbled away from the waterfront where most of the town's population had congregated for our departure. We managed to get under the big, new bridge without hitting any of the piers, and were off on what proved to be an almost total disaster of a trip. The river was at its highest level — it was the peak of the rainly season — and its chocolate mass was fast flowing and full of flotsam such as whole clumps of jungle trees and branches. We felt decidedly unstable in the canoe, a mere sneeze would probably·toss us into that soup, with all its well-advertised horrors — electric eels, prianhas, alligators, and sting-rays.

We had foolishly set off very late in the day with only three hours of daylight left but we had intended to camp a few miles downstream. However when we began to look for a site in the rapidly fading light we realized that there wasn't even any land let alone a clearing — merely flooded jungle everywhere. The sun went down and there we were paddling in a wobbly craft in total darkness. We tried to nose the canoe into the flooded jungle to tie up there but the current forced the canoe under some low branches and bearly capsized us, ants fell on us while animals shrieked and leapt in the tree tops. After that it seemed almost nice to be back in the middle of the river.

Finally, we found a few branches from a submerged tree on an even more submerged island to tie up to for the night. A very dangerous situation — any floating tree could have barged into us during the night. We were more concerned about what might come slithering out of the river. Then it began to rain torrentially for the next ten hours. There we sat until dawn: Frozen, hungry, soaked, boiling water, flashing our light in panic and getting drunk on rum.

Well, we survived the night and for the next three weeks we paddled hard, got drenched, went hungry, watched our skins rot, got eaten by mosquitoes and went for two or three days at a time without seeing any dry land. Finally when we were offered a lift with a motor boat we accepted with undignified haste! And the fact the I went on to do three more canoe trips (and would do another tomorrow) shows that, despite these beginnings, something had attracted me. I hope that the following advice will encourage you to try a trip of this sort, and avoid your having to learn purely by error.

CHOICE OF RIVER

There's really no reason why all the Amazonian tributaries can't be travelled by canoe, however access is difficult and so are rapids. Although I don't really believe that previous canoeing experience is essential for these trips (within three days you'll be good), it *is* essential if you are likely to encounter rapids near the beginning. I would recommend a quiet river for the first trip for the following reasons. You will gain skill at canoeing without the risk of getting tested in white water. And, as there are no rapids, the river is likely to be navigable and fairly populated. Therefore if it proves to be too much, or something goes wrong, you'll have a good chance of cadging a lift on a river boat, or help from the locals. In these relaxed conditions you'll have plenty of time to perfect fishing and hunting techniques, get used to sleeping in the jungle, and gain confidence in all aspects of canoeing. An ideal river for a first canoe trip is the Guaporé — and I'll describe that in detail later.

I have met other travellers who have canoed down the Amazon from Peru to the Atlantic, but I personally couldn't face such a trip. The river is too wide and too populated to be very interesting. It would degenerate into a monotonous paddle (in pretty choppy conditions) without enough compensations in terms of wildlife, isolation or visual interest. The same can probably be said of the rivers Madeira, Negro and Purus. Even the Branco, while an attractive river during the dry season, has long, long stretches where the river merges with the sky on the horizon, the current slows to a crawl and the river widens to a kilometer. Personally I find that a psychological killer; I like a fairly narrow river, with a few twists and turns, and a fairly scattered population to keep my mind off the paddling. Fewer people also means more wildlife, and that for me is the greatest reward of a trip of this sort.

After you've had your baptism on a quiet river you can then get a good map and hunt for something more adventurous. Maps from INPA (Amazon Research Institute) in Manaus are the best that I've found, and they let you make photocopies. When looking for a river watch out for rapids and waterfalls. A few rapids are fun and break the monotony, but too many become a chore and increase the risk. I travelled down a tributary of the river Teles Pires with an Australian friend and it was unmitigated slog with rapid after rapid, and some of them very dangerous. (Waterfalls are almost impossible to get round with the very heavy local canoes.) So check carefully for rapids on the map and take into account that for every ten they mark there'll be another two or three that they won't. Try to find a river that has access by road to somewhere on its upper reaches — preferably with a village or town where you stand a good chance of buying a canoe. Somewhere downstream (always go downstram unless you're really trying to prove something) there should be a road back to civilization. The sad truth is that there are not many tributaries that meet these requirements. A lot of potentially lovely (though hairy) tributaries like the Juruena, Roosevelt, or Upper Zingu are too difficult to get to with a canoe, or without a village at the right place to be able to buy one. The Teles Pires is an exception, and I'll also talk about that later.

TYPE OF CANOE

Ideally of course, if I were wealthy, I'd take a fibergalss Canadian canoe to Brazil and get a truck to take me to the river of my choice. They are so light and portable that they would be ideal for getting through (or around) rapids. However, here are the cheap alternatives: The dugout, the plank-built canoe and the metal canoe. The latter look lovely, and work beautifully with a motor, but are brutes to paddle. Also if you are unlucky enough to hole one repairs would be very tricky. The dugout is the most widely used craft and for quiet rivers they are light to paddle and alright once you get used to their wobbliness. However, as they sit low in the water, especially with two people and provisions, they are not good in choppy water. Of course the freeboard can be increased by fixing an extra 15 cm. plank around the gunnale. The plank-built canoe is heavy to paddle but more stable and can carry more. After all there's no great rush anyway, and the confidence a plank canoe gives makes up for any lack of speed. These canoes have to meet waves before they ship water, and they allow you to paddle standing up when your bum gets sore, fool about and even dive off them.

MAKING A PLANK CANOE

The method was shown to me at Vila Bela on the upper Guaporé, by Odorico Da Silva, and I have subsequently made two others by this method for use on the Verde and Teles Pires and, although they look crude and basic they never gave me a moments worry and seem to get stronger the longer they are in the water. The advantage of knowing how to make your own canoe is that even if you can't find one for sale there'll usually be a sawmill nearby.

Briefy, to make a 5 m. canoe, a good size for two people and provisions for two months, you need: 6 hardwood planks; 4 of 1½ cm. thickness for the sides, and 2 of 2 cm. thickness for the bottom (I'm talking of planks with a width of 50 cm.); nails: 2 dozen 7½ cm. long and 8 dozen 5 cm. long; a large

HOW TO BUILD 5 M. 2 PEOPLE & PROVISIONS PLANK CANOE

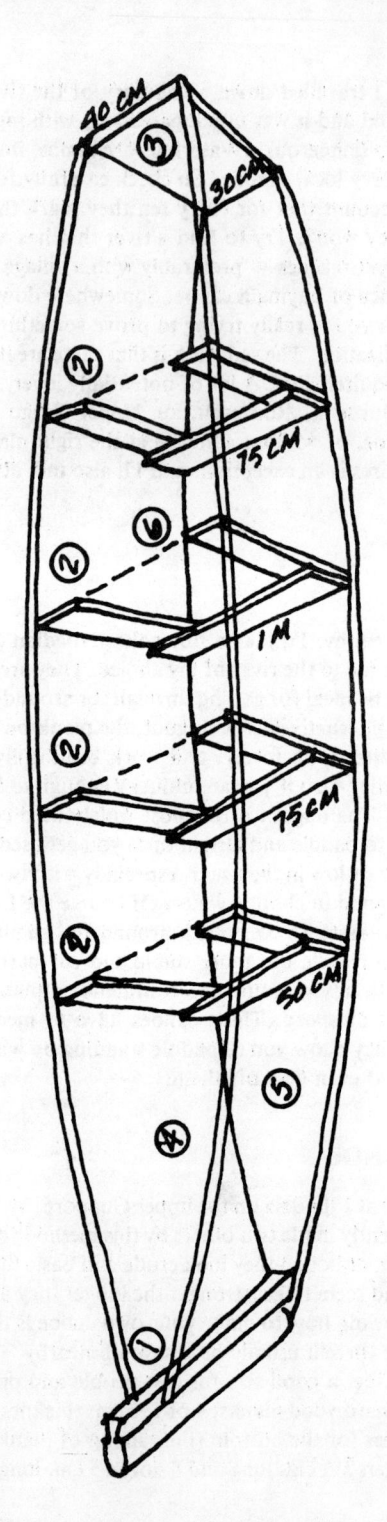

① BOW PEICE 65×15×15 CM ⌒ KEYHOLE SHAPED ② 4 FRAMES 6×2½ CM EACH LAPPED, GLUED & NAILED ③ STERN PEICE 30-40 CM ×4 CM ④ SIDE PLANKS 1½ × 50 CM ⑤ BOTTOM PLANKS 2×50 CM ⑥ TEMPORARY SPREADING STRUTS

ⓐ SPACE FRAMES, BOW & STERN PEICES ON GROUND FOR CANOE SHAPE. BEND & NAIL SIDE PLANKS TO THESE, TRIMMED TO BOW & STERN ⓑ TURN OVER, TRIM BOTTOM PLANKS TO SIDES, NAIL ⓒ CRAM FLAX INTO ALL JOINTS, SOAK WITH HEATED PITCH.

bundle of straw (flax) and 3 kg. of pitch. Perhaps the job could be improved by using screws, but my canoes never had that treat. Buy these latter items in the last large town you are going to pass through because they probably won't be obtainable locally in a sawmill village.

PROVISIONS

Basically you need the following items:

Gun. Either a .22 caliber rifle or a shotgun, or ideally both. The legal position on firearms in Amazonia seems to vary from place to place. In Cuiabá and Porto Velho nobody would sell me a gun. In Manaus I went to the police and they sent me to a local gun shop where the owner let me pick what I wanted, then got me all the documents I needed within 24 hours and at no extra charge. I've forgotten the name of the shop unfortunately, but the police station is downtown, near the port, and they are helpful. To travel around without firearm documents means certain confiscation of the weapon. A single shot .22 rifle, or small caliber shotgun, costs about 90 dollars. Buy all the ammunition in Manaus too, it costs treble in the wilds. Get the type of firearm which can be dismantled to fit in your luggage until you get to the river. Get gun-oil and a cleaning rod to prevent rust. You can usually sell your gun at the end of your trip for a profit.

Fishing tackle. Make sure it is heavy duty: 300 meters of 20 kg. test strength line, 50 large hooks and a dozen small, a few weights, and a few meters of ordinary fencing wire. Always use a length of twisted wire between the hook and the line. Ordinary, thin nylon cord makes good lines and is much stronger than nylon fishing line.

Miscellaneous. A machete for cutting firewood and clearing camp sites. Mosquito netting and a hammock. A large plastic sheet to camp under if it rains (5 m. square), 15 m. of nylon rope for use in rapids, kerosene lamps, torches, batteries, 5 liters of kerosene, matches, knives (a fish filleting knife is useful) a blanket because it gets surprisingly cold at night, long sleeve shirts, basketball sneekers, two spare paddles (the market at Manaus has beautiful cheap paddles — buy them there); a piece of old inner tube or gum boot because that's the best thing for starting a fire with damp wood, a very large frying pan, two saucepans, coffee pot.

Food. Just like the Brazilians you will be eating the basic staples of rice and beans supplemented by what fish you catch and the game you shoot. Also spaghetti, coffee, lots of sugar and salt, assorted spices to liven it all up, big tin of powdered milk, cooking oil, flour to coat the fish and lots of goodies to treat yourself occasionally — boiled sweets, booze, drinking chocolate, chewing gum etc.

Compass. Once you learn to use the compass it takes all the fear out of jungle walking — it's so easy to lose your bearings without it.

Medicine kit. Anti-malarials, scissors, pincers, plasters, bandages, antiseptic creams, dusting powder, temporary fillings, antibiotics, vitamin pills etc.

DANGERS AND PRECAUTIONS

Generally I found most of the well publicized myths of Amazonia to be greatly exaggerated. I swam frequently and no piranhas attacked, but don't go out too far, make sure you're not bleeding and avoid stagnant pools where the food supply may be scarce.

Alligators, anacondas and jaguars are generally even more frightened of you than you are of them. Keep a fire burning all night if you want — it is comforting, but even if it goes out nothing will happen; I've only seen seven snakes in eleven months in Amazonia and five of them were swimming.

Sting rays are a big danger, and it is easy to step on one when you get out of the canoe. The wound they leave is ghastly and excruciatingly painful apparently. Prod the area with the paddle before you step out, and walk with a shuffle through the water to scare off any rays lying in the mud. So if you keep a watchful eye for snakes and sting rays you'd be very unfortunate indeed to get bitten or attacked by any of the wildlife.

RAPIDS

Rapids obviously need approaching with caution. When you hear one ahead always stop well upstream of it and go and scout. You can then decide if it's passable or needs a more careful approach. With one person on the bank, anchored and paying out the rope, and the other wading (or swimming) holding the bow of the canoe you can get round the edge of all but the fiercest rapids. Unfortunately the local canoes and the plank canoes are so heavy that any long portage is almost impossbile especially on rough terrain. Be aware that if the canoe turns over you'll probably make it to the bank but you'll lose almost everything you need for survival. At all times wear a belt pouch with some anti-malarials, fishing tackle, compass and matches (in plastic bags of course) to make sure you have the basics if the worst happens.

You'll meet people from time to time. Make a point of stopping for a chat even if you don't even feel like it. They'll tell you of conditions ahead, the next house etc. and such information could be crucial if you need to know where the nearest help lies (anyway you'll get a cup of coffee at the very least).

HUNTING AND FISHING

As I said before your diet will be of the basic rice, beans and spaghetti supplemented by what you fish and shoot. Fishing is easy and is best with pieces of fish as bait cast into faster flowing or eddying water. Quieter, deeper water will produce too many piranha, which while good eating are a bit of a bore to get off the hook without getting bitten, especially in the dark. Night lines tied to saplings often produce large fish. Even if you don't rate fishing as a sport you'll enjoy it in these rivers. It's so easy, the fish are often so big (they'll break your line often) and such good eating.

I'm not normally a great meat eater but within a month of being on the river I experienced a carnivorous lust for juicy, bloody meat which was probably a desire to escape from fish. The most sought after animals for meat are the tapir (much too big for less than six or seven people), wild pigs, capybara, small deer, turtles and monkeys if you have the heart. Wild pigs shouldn't be passed up if you get a chance. You'll come across their wallowing places along the sides of creeks. They spend the heat of the day in the mud so you should get into position before 9 A.M. Capybaras often dive into the water when they see you. Tie up the canoe 50 m. downstream and sit quietly and they'll usually reappear 15 minutes later. Avoid the old ones as they are pretty rank. Most of our meat came from ducks, bush turkeys and other large feathered friends which are abundant and provide a good meal for two without waste.

INSECTS

Life in Amazonia would be a paradise if it weren't for our six legged friends. I suppose every rose has its thorns, but they are a bit numerous. Certain times of year are better than others, and that depends on the rainy season. To the south of the main Amazon river the rainy season is from October to April, and to the north of the main river from April to August. Avoid any trip in the rainy season — it means hours of torrential rain, wet hammocks, no dry firewood, scarce game and more insects. I also believe that the very beginning and end of the rainy season are the worst for malaria. Therefore go in july to September in the south, and December to March in the north. Watch out for the leaf-cutter ants because they have a taste for nylon. In one night they carried away half of my pack so everything fell out of the bottom when I picked it up!

DISEASE

Malaria is the big danger. In 1980 we both came down with it, fortunately two days after we left the river. I was taking double-dosage Maloprim, and he was taking double-dosage Fansidar preventive. We never missed a dose, and as they are recommended drugs we can only assume that under certain conditions nothing is going to give 100% protection. I got two strains of malaria: Vivax and Falciperum, and I got weak so fast I would have been in serious trouble in the jungle. However there were two factors that serve as warnings. First, we had gotten physically run down so our resistance was probably lowered. Second, our trip extended into the first month of the rainy season. Avoid that period, and consult local specialists about the drug of the moment.

THE RIVER GUAPORÉ

An ideal river for starters. Begin at Vila Bela (also known as Mato Grosso), which you can reach by bus from Cuiabá via Pontes e Lacerda. There are two hotels, provisions can be bought there and you stand a good chance of finding a second-hand dugout to buy, or Odorico da Silva will build you a plank canoe for about one hundred dollars (he lives on the opposite bank). Alternatively, there's a sawmill and you can build you own. The Upper Guaporé is a lovely river — narrow and twisting with the occasional ranch opened on its banks. If you stop at meal times you'll get a great meal at the cowboys' canteen. There are no rapids on the Guaporé between Vila Bela and Guajará-Mirim about 1,600 km. downstream. The river forms the boundary between Brazil and Bolivia for much of its length. I canoed along the Guaporé for three weeks before I accepted a lift from a river boat. There is a scattered population of friendly people (as all the Brazilain river dwellers are) who will always give you a place to hang your hammocks. As they'll offer you food try to arrive with some game or fish as payment. Even better take a poloroid camera and thank them with presents. Any articles from your country such as coins postcards, will be treasured. A few boats travel the river every month so when you get tired they'll give you a tow and will get you to Guajaré-Mirim where there are roads back to Cuiabá or up to Manaus. Although the Guaporé valley is going to be opened up very soon by a new road and cattle ranching, it is still a river with long stretches of virgin jungle and fairly abundant wildlife. How long this will continue I don't know.

THE TELES PIRES

To get to the Teles Pires go 500 km. due north from Cuiabá on the road to Santarem to the town of Sinop. There you will find dozens of sawmills where you can make a canoe and shops to buy all provisions. I've been back twice and made two canoes in the premises of the largest sawmill. When the canoe is complete find a truck to take you to the river about 25 km. away. The Teles Pries is a wild river and has plenty of rapids of varying intensity. Don't do it as a first canoe trip. Originally Andrea and I had wanted to canoe the full length to Jacareacanga on the Tapajos River, nearly 1,600 km. where we planned to take the Trans-amazonian highway out. However after twenty rapids, 640 km. and seven weeks we met our Waterloo at the Villeray rapid, 3 km. of unpassable cataracts, falls and danger. We abandoned the canoe and walked for nine days until we got to Paranaita. With a fiberglass canoe the portage would have been possible.

With a heavy plank canoe limit your trip to the section between Sinop and the area near Alta Floresta. Taken at a leisurely pace you'll have a few weeks on the river, will pass through 15 rapids, see only one or two homestead, lots of wildlife, and experience Amazonia close to its virgin state. You'll like it, but I repeat: Do an easier river first.

Some final words. Organizing and carrying out a trip of this sort would be difficult and dangerous without some knowledge of Portuguese. Spanish is a great help and having that as a base you'll pick up Portuguese very quickly. Nobody will speak English and you'll miss out on so much if you can't communicate (it's also important for safety's sake to understand warnings and advice).

Two other quiet rivers to canoe down that should be interesting are the Arinos (between the Cuidabá — Santarem road and Porto Dos Gauchos), and the river Paraguay south of Cuiabá.

Bananas and Hunting Dogs *A party of adventurers enters a remote and previously unexplored valley in deepest Amazonia. There they discover a small community of primitive people living a life without awareness of anything or anyone beyond the unpeopled green forests and winding rivers of their homeland. Yet there are two inconsistencies in the lifestyle of these previously uncontacted folk who know nothing of an outside world: They grow bananas and they keep hunting dogs! "So what?" you ask. Well, we are told that bananas originated in Asia: Later they were introduced to tropical Africa and it was only relatively recently that Portuguese and Spanish explorers took them to South America. And the dogs? They were introduced from somewhere outside that continent, too. Then how is it that small tribes of shy, secretive people, scattered throughout that vast wilderness, separated geographically by journeys that would take them weeks, isolated (it seems reasonable to expect) for centuries, if not thousands of years how is it that they all keep hunting dogs and grow bananas?*

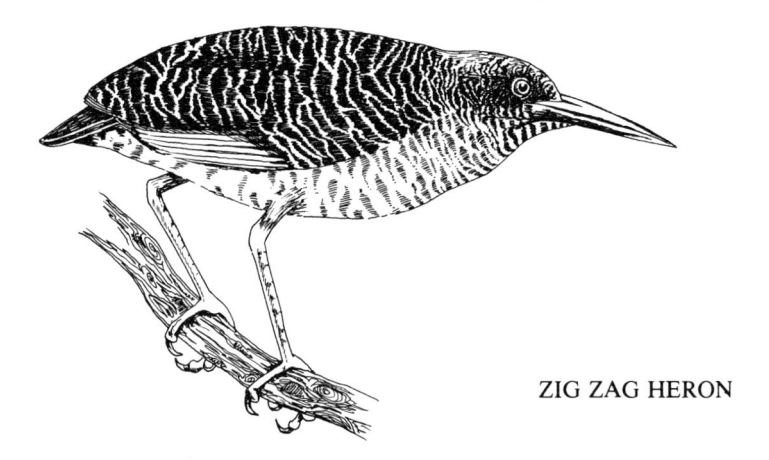

ZIG ZAG HERON

MAP NUMBER 5

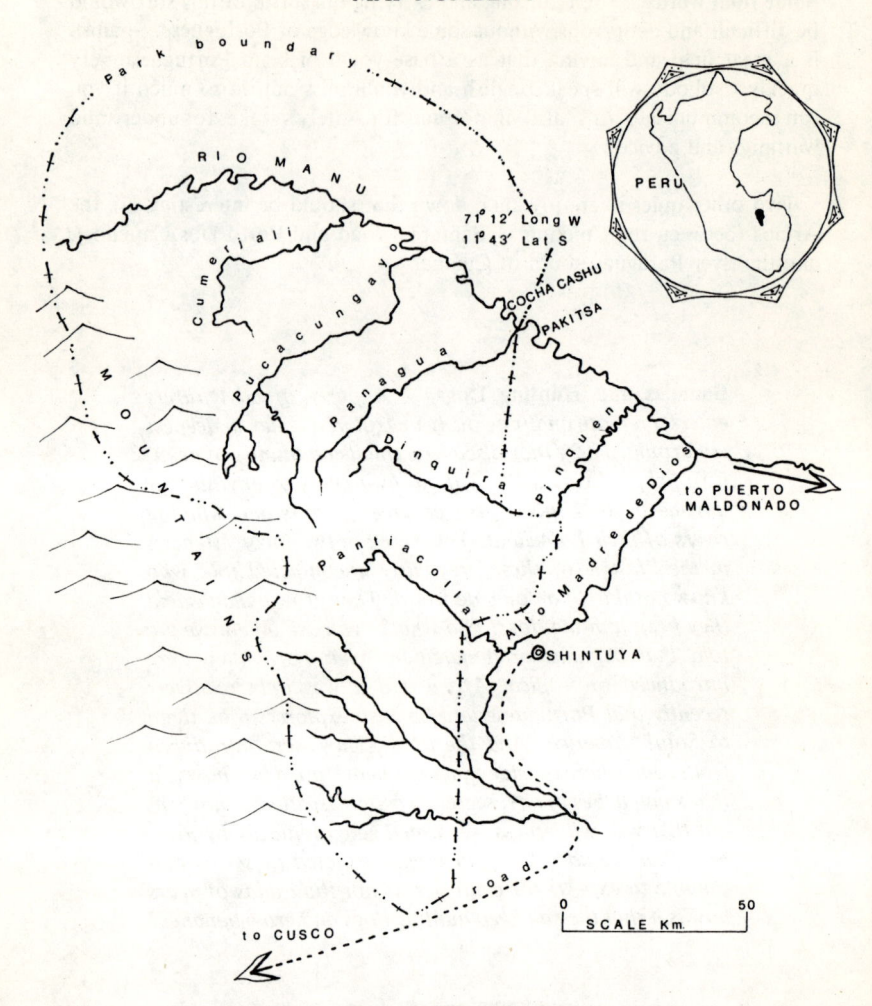

Peru

Manu National Park

Manu National Park in southeast Peru extends from the heights of the Andes down into the humid, forest-clad lowlands of the Amazon Basin. Indeed, the term *national park* can be somewhat misleading, as in this context it's used to describe an area that is larger than Northern Ireland, is 90 percent unexplored, has no roads, is inhabited by several tribes of Indians (many of whom have not yet been contacted by modern man), and has the distinction of containing some of the richest, least-disturbed, and least-known parts of the Amazonian ecosystem.

To reach even the edge of the park involves two back-breaking and hair-raising days trucking along dirt roads through the Andes from Cuzco to Shintuya, where the road ends. This is followed by another couple of days of river travel down the Alto Madre de Dios and up the Manu River to a small guard post called Pakitsa in a jungle clearing on the riverbank just a few kilometers outside the northeastern boundary of the park.

Tanis and I arrived at Pakitsa on a steaming-hot day in early June. With us we had an Avon Redseal inflatable rubber dinghy powered by a 9-h.p. Yamaha outboard engine, a three months' supply of dehydrated foodstuffs, 70 gallons of gas that we'd brought all the way from Cuzco, and a letter from the Ministry of Agriculture in Lima granting us permission to travel freely within the park collecting plants and taking photographs.

It's the job of the guards to keep unauthorized persons such as skin hunters, gold prospectors, and missionaries out of the park and also to accompany and look after visiting scientists from a small biological research station just upriver from Pakitsa. They greeted the news that we intended to go off exploring without a guide with shocked disbelief. Latin courtesy was almost forgotten for the first hour or two after our arrival as our hosts, concerned for our welfare, described the dangers to which we would be exposing ourselves: There were snakes and pumas and other wild animals, we might become lost, ill, or drown in the fast-flowing rivers but most likely we would meet up with hostile Indians. Machigengas, Yaminawas, and Amahuacas are the names of just three of the Indian tribes living in and around the park and they are officially described as being "restless" at present. From what we could gather this meant that they were in a state of war with each other and that the Amahuacas in particular were in the habit of raiding the villages of the Machigengas and are also quite likely to attack any intruders into their territory.

Alarming though this information was we had no intention of changing our plans at this late stage and sought to assure the guards that we would take no unnecessary risks by entering known Amahuaca territory nor remain camped for long in any one place. We also pointed out that a man and a woman in a small boat would be far less likely to be regarded as a threat by primitive people than would the more conventional expedition party that usually consists of canoes full of hairy men, native guides, and boatmen, all bristling with guns and knives. Eventually we won our way and were told that we could leave the next day for the biological research station at Cocha Cashu (a small oxbow lake) and from there we could go wherever we pleased. As if to convince us of the wildness of the country we were in, the guards told us that we would see primitive uncontacted Indians the very next day, even before we reached Cocha Cashu: Just a week before our arrival three women had emerged from the jungle and camped on the riverbank. It was thought that they had come to the Manu down the Panagua valley but nobody knew to what tribe they belonged. To demonstrate friendliness two of the guards had paddled past their camp in a canoe and left a shirt, a length of mosquito netting, and some food on the beach where the women could collect them. We were warned that if we saw them it would be unwise to stop as there could be men hiding in the background.

At dawn the next morning we motored away upstream in our grossly overladen boat feeling both nervous and elated. Certainly the scene viewed from the middle of the wide, muddy river looked idyllic rather than dangerous. To the left rose a steep bank of red earth and to the right lay a wide beach of golden sand. A flock of scarlet and blue macaws flew overhead and settled in a palm tree, driving away a pair of toucans and a heron. Three turtles sunning themselves on a log dropped into the water with a nicely synchronized plop as we came alongside. We pulled the boat into the beach, turned off the engine, and walked across the sand. A group of caimans that had been lying motionless along the shoreline sprang to life and splashed into the shallows. The river curled away out of sight both behind and ahead of us and our view to either side of the river channel stopped at the solid wall of leaves, branches, and tangled lianas, that dense barrier of prolific vegetation that conceals the cool, airy interior and lofty green mansions of virgin tropical rain forest.

At midday, making painfully slow progress against the fast current, we rounded a bend and saw one of the Indian women emerge from the bushes on the near bank. She was dark skinned and long haired, and she crouched low as if ready to turn and flee into the forest. Keeping the boat away from the shore we waved and smiled and soon she was joined by a second woman, naked except for some green material wrapped around her waist — the mosquito net the guards had left. The women clapped their hands and shouted and ran along through the jungle beside us. It was a full five minutes before we left them behind and then we saw a conical grass hut on a beach and the third woman appeared. This one was young with a short haircut and she wore a tattered man's shirt — the other gift from the park guards. When it became apparent that we were not going to stop, she ran along the sand keeping pace with us just as the other two had done.

Months later back in the city we heard more about these women from a German scientist who made contact with them. They were on their own, perfectly harmless and friendly but nothing was established about their origin as the scientist's Indian guides couldn't understand the language they spoke. They live at a surprisingly primitive level without tools, weapons, or boats. They don't have fire but eat raw what they gather or catch with their hands, a diet that includes fish, small animals, and turtles.

Cocha Cashu is ½ km. from the main river. The research station consists of a group of wooden houses on the water's edge dwarfed by huge trees on three sides. Here we met Brigitte, a biologist from West Germany studying giant otters, her assistant Michael, and their guard and guide Armando. They, too, had a boat (by a curious coincidence it was an Avon inflatable model, powered by a Yamah outboard engine, almost the same outfit as our own) and it was decided that all five of us would make an expedition upriver in the two boats to do a bit of exploring and search for otters.

Two weeks passed and we made the adjustment to jungle life. By this time we were well inside the park and had made journeys up two small unnamed side rivers. We saw no more people but at one remote spot 10 km. from the main river we found human footprints on a beach, clear and sharp edged among the tracks of the deer and peccaries and caimans. Our "Man Friday" had been accompanied by a small child and it was evident that the pair had come to this spot to search for turtles' nests in the sand. They'd found one, sat down and eaten the twenty or so eggs raw, leaving the shells scattered around like broken ping-pong balls. After this we made a point of looking for evidence of humans and sometimes found it, usually in the form of a footprint in the soft mud or finger-snapped twigs in the forest, marking someone's way among the trees.

This jungle was full of surprises, not the least of which were the cold spells when the temperature would suddenly plummet to 15° C. or even lower and remain there for twenty-four hours or so. At those times the gray skies, cool winds, and the conspicuous absence of birds and beasts made it easy to forget that we were in lowland tropical rain forest. Unfortunately, though, these dismal periods did nothing to inhibit the activities of the biting insects that were on or near the Manu River in numbers we would not have believed possible had we not been forced to endure their attentions. Throughout the daylight hours we were tormented by tiny blackflies, whose bite brings up a subcutaneous blood blister that itches appallingly. Once we counted 170 of these blisters on one of Tanis's ankles. At night we were besieged by mosquitoes. In another experiment I put my hand outside the mosquito net and after sixty seconds there were eleven of them sucking my blood. What, we wondered, did they all feed on when there were no people around?

It was an odd feature of the insect fauna that on the side rivers mosquitoes were often entirely absent, a fact that made life much easier for us when we traveled these small meandering streams, with their clear greenish waters and borders of golden sands. Our nights around the camp fire were delightful, but for our fears about hostile Indians. We were in unexplored country and nothing is known about the people who live there.

One day on a river called the Pucacungayo we noticed a trail leading from the waterside up into the forest, followed it, and walked straight into an Indian camp. No Indians were at home, but they'd left only very recently: A palm frond had been placed in the ground with the unwilted leaves carefully trimmed to make it a semicircular shape, which meant that the owners hadn't deserted their camp and would be returning. There were six low, thatched huts, each just high enough for four or five people to sit or sleep beneath, and there were neatly constructed palm-leaf sleeping mats standing up against the trees. A wide, cleared trail led away into the forest and branches had been broken and laid across it like the rungs of a horizontal ladder, for what purpose I've no idea. Armando said it was a village of "wild Yaminawas" and he was very uneasy. In fact, he couldn't wait to get out of the place, while the rest of us, slightly dazed by our discovery, took out the cameras and proceeded to photograph the scene like tourists on a regular sightseeing trip. Back in the boats we wondered if any of the occupants of the place had been hidden among the trees watching us.

On our return to Cocha Cashu we said goodbye to our friends and set off down the Manu headed for the Pinquen River.

It was July, well into the dry season, and the waters were very low. In places we had to pull the boat over long stretches of shingly shallows where the river was no more than knee deep. Here we saw the big toothless catfish called *sungaro,* a meter and more in length and sometimes as many as a dozen visible at one time. There was nothing to fear from the catfish; they would swim downstream of us and if we remained still would make tentative expeditions in our direction. But there were stingrays too hidden in the mud and sand of these shallow waters and we always shuffled our feet to give plenty of warning of our approach. All along this river were great flocks of macaws. To see even one of these birds in the wild is a dazzling spectacle but fifty or more of them in one eyeful just numbs the senses.

In this undisturbed land there was plenty of wildlife to see. Deer, tapirs, peccaries, capybaras, and sometimes ocelots and giant otters would watch us from the riverbanks, more curious than afraid unless we ventured too near. During just one week we identified seven species of monkey without even searching for them (and that left at least another six species we did not encounter). In fact, some creatures were a bit too bold for our peace of mind, such was the huge furry spider that found its way into Tanis's rucksack and the jaguar that strolled into our camp one night to have a look around. That animal was a heavy breather. Tanis heard the snuffling and grunting and thinking that it was me snoring she prodded my hammock to shut me up.

Another night we were awakened by a terrible splashing and thumping and, realizing that something was attacking our boat, seized the flashlights

Tapir
The markings on the coat of the young serve as camouflage and are eventually lost. The adult is the size of a donkey. Tapirs whistle like birds.

and rushed down to the water. Our rubber dinghy was bobbing up and down surrounded by caimans, their eyes glowing like coals in the flashlight beam, but they soon submerged and surfaced some distance away to watch us. Only one remained, whose shape I could make out close against the side of the boat. I called out to Tanis: "It's OK, he's only a little one." Then I realized with horror that I was looking at just the head; the body was beneath the surface, all 4 m. of it! Clamped firmly between the reptile's grizzly jaws was the rope that secured all our precious equipment. The end of it had been carelessly left dangling in the water. It was a heavy climber's rope with a breaking strain of several thousand pounds. Tanis is always ready with suggestions on these occasions. "Hit it on the head with something," she instructed, and I obediently picked up a large piece of driftwood, crept down to the riverside, bopped the animal on the snout and then ran up the bank in a panic, imagining it was right behind me snapping at my ankles. But I needn't have worried. It simply released the rope and swam away to surface a minute or so later in midstream as the others had done. Presumably the big caiman had decided that our boat was an enemy and have been endeavoring to beat the living daylights out of it.

On a small stream called the Dinquira the scenery and vegetation was superficially similar to the other rivers we'd seen but the insect fauna was different again. Large sweat bees in extraordinary numbers were out during the day and moths at night. Sweat bees don't sting or bite; they just land on the skin and either get hopelessly entangled in hair or attempt to crawl into the nearest orifice — ear, eye, or nostril. At night the moths were so numerous that we had to sit away from the camp fire to prevent our hot tea from becoming moth soup. From there we could watch moths and lovely fireflies with amber lights on their heads and flashing green lights on their bodies committing suicide in the flames.

Eventually we became aware that we were being followed and spied on by Indians. We were just a couple of valleys away from the spot where an expedition was massacred some years before. The knowledge that Indian attacks almost invariablly occur at dawn had us up and about lighting fires at 3:30 every morning, listening with suspicion and alarm to the hoots, whistles, and cries emanating from the darkness of the forest. Four days of this was enough and we turned around and headed back downstream.

The first incident on the downriver trip was a collision with a fallen tree. It tore a hole in the boat and we spent another night of acute anxiety wondering if we were still being watched while the boat was under repair. Then there was an electrical storm that lasted for sixteen hours and seemed to us as if the world was about to come to an end. After the rains finally ceased and the clouds dispersed, the river rose 1 m. then sank back to its previous level. Quite unpredictably the next evening it rose 4 m. in two hours and flooded our camp in the darkness. We lost all of our cooking gear and eating utensils that time. Not one pot, plate, cup, spoon, or fork remained. The rusty tin can used for bailing out the boat proved excellent to cook in and from this we ate rice and beans with our fingers. But at that stage in the journey the incident was nothing more than a minor inconvenience. We'd long ago used all our sugar, flour, and oil, eaten most of our dried dinners, smoked most of our cigarettes, and were then rolling the tobacco in air-mail writing paper. We were resigned to a very basic standard of living. It was late August, the rainy season was due, and we were heading back home.

Our return trip took us down the Manu and onto the wide, fast-flowing Madre de Dios River for a journey of over 150 km. Before very long we came to people, little encampments of gold prospectors digging up the gravel beds and the sandbanks and straightening up from their work to stare as our strange-looking little outfit sailed past. Now there were no animals to be seen. They were in hiding, a sad contrast to the Manu National Park. Drifting much of the way to conserve gas, the journey lasted six days, taking us past the mouths of the Rio Blanco, Rio Azul, and Rio Colorado. It was six days of beautiful misty mornings merging into blazing hot afternoons, and evening camps on shingle beaches where we talked incessantly about hot showers and comfortable beds, fresh food, glasses of ice-cold beer, and news from home.

Then came the afternoon when we arrived at Labarinto, a tiny frontier settlement with a road connection to Puerto Maldonado, a town with an airfield and flights to Cuzco. We moored our boat among the row of dugout canoes beneath a steep clay bank watched by a large crowd of Labarinto's inhabitants, more people than we'd seen all together for months. With something of a shock we realized that our trip was now suddenly over.

Leaving Tanis in the boat I climbed the bank and entered the dusty heat of the little town. Dilapidated wooden shacks, fruit stalls, hardware stores, and bars lined the main street. A wide, red-dirt track disappeared into the jungle 200 m. away and there were trucks and motor bikes, dogs, pigs, chickens, and children, Andean Indians, and miners in noisy groups, most of them reeling drunk. Piles of refuse lay everywhere — rotting fruit, broken bottles, and rusty tins, with the overwhelming stench of gasoline and garbage. It was all very confusing. I found a truck driver who was leaving for Puerto Maldonado in an hour's time and he said he would take us there for 1,000 soles (about $3 U.S.). Hastily we began shoving our belongings into kit bags and sweated up and down the slippery bank piling them into the back of the truck. The last item was our faithful inflatable boat and when we had it aboard we were ready to depart. Throughout the whole operation Tanis had been very quiet and now she looked distinctly sad.

"What's the matter?" I asked. "Aren't you looking forward to all those things we've been missing for the last three months?"

"Not very much," she replied. "I wish we were still on the river."

And so did I.

About the Authors

When Tanis and Martin Jordan submitted a brief and exciting manuscript for the first volume in this series on South American river trips, the book was already being printed. After reading the account of their rubber boat being attacked by caimans, I thought seriously about telephoning the printer and having him stop the presses.

Instead I exuberantly offered them carte blanche to write a book, hoping there were more tales and adventures. The Jordans seemed shy and noncommittal about the project, typically English in fact. But as soon as I walked into their north London flat I knew it would all work out.

One wall was lined with every possible type of book on jungles, the tropics, and explorations. A mysteriously lit jungle scene, painted on an enormous canvas, dominated the opposite wall. Against a third wall: guinea pigs! Cages full of fat, friendly fellows. Martin and I winked at each other as we sat down to a stew that Tanis explained was not *cuy* (Peruvians think these rodents delicious), but venison.

Tanis and Martin met while both working as hair dressers. Now Tanis owns and operates the neighborhood beauty parlor with her mother while Martin is a part-time construction foreman. In addition to drawing and painting, Martin spends his off hours making gallons (imperial) of delicious wines.

Their mutual interests include studying (Tanis, psychology; Martin, biology), body building, scuba diving, and Bushido, a form of unarmed combat. Wildlife conservation, in the face of uncontrolled human population growth, pollution, and deforestation worldwide, is their main concern.

Tanis and Martin have been traveling together for fourteen years now. They've toured the Sahara, the Atlas mountains, and the West Indies in addition to four trips (two years in all) to South American jungles.

Says Martin, "Between river trips we often decide we're going to visit some other part of the world like Borneo, New Guinea, or the Antarctic, but we always end up going back to South America. I suppose we're in some kind of a rut!"

88 BUTTERFLY

Bibliography

Asheshov, Anna. *The Gold in the River.* London: Hodder & Stoughton, 1975.
Bates, Henry W. *Naturalist on the River Amazon.* New York: Dover, 1975.
Bates, Marston. *The Forest and the Sea.* New York: Vintage Book, 1965.
The Land and Wildlife of South America. Alexandria, Va.: Time-Life Books, 1964.
Brooks, John. *The South American Handbook.* Bath: Trade & Travel Publications (Rand McNally U.S. distributers), annual.
Cameron, Donald. *Sons of El Dorado.* London: Longmans, 1970.
Charriere, Henri. *Papillon.* London: Hart Davis Macgibbon, 1971, and New York: William Morrow & Co., 1970.
De Civrieux, M. *Watunna: An Orinoco Creation Cycle.* San Francisco: North Point Press, 1980.
Dorst, Jean. *South and Central America: A Natural History.* New York: Random House, 1967.
Evans, D.L. and Counter, S.A. *I Sought My Brother.* Cambridge, Mass.: M.I.T. Press, 1981
Fiedler, Arkady. *The River of Singing Fish.* London: Hodder & Stoughton, 1951.
Goulding, Michael. *The Fishes in the Forest.* Berkeley, Ca.: University of California Press, 1980.
Guppy, Nicholas. *Wai Wai.* London: John Murray, 1958.
A Young Man's Journey. London: John Murray, 1973.
Haverschmidt, Francois. *Birds of Surinam.* London: Oliver & Boyd, 1968.
Junk, Dr. W. *Man and Fisheries on the Amazon River.* The Hague, 1981.
Kingland, Rosemary. *A Saint among Savages.* London: Collins, 1980.
Kloos, Peter. *The Akuriyo of Surinam.* Copenhagen: IWGIA, 1977.
Man, John: *The Amazon.* Alexandria, Va.: Time-Life Books, 1973.
Morrison, Tony. *The Andes.* Alexandria, Va.: Time-Life Books, 1976.
Moser, Brian and Donald Taylor. *The Cocaine Eaters.* London: Longmans, 1965.
Moser, Don. *The Central American Jungles.* Alexandria, Va.: Time-Life Books 1976.
Perry, Richard. *The World of the Jaguar.* David & Charles Ltd, 1970, and New York: Taplinger.
Richards, P.W. *The Tropical Rainforest.* Cambridge: Cambridge University Press, 1952.
The Life of the Jungle. New York: McGraw-Hill Book Co., 1970.
Schneebaum, Tobias. *Keep the River on Your Right.* London: Jonathan Cape Ltd, 1970, and New York: Grove Press, 1969.
Schulz, J.P. *Sea Turtles Nesting in Surinam.* Amsterdam: Rijksmuseum of Natural History, 1975.
Schwabe, Calvin W. *Unmentionable Cuisine.* Charlottesville: University of Virginia, 1979.
Shoumatoff, Alex. *The Rivers Amazon.* San Francisco: Sierra Club Books, 1978.

Smith, Anthony. *Mato Grosso.* London: M. Joseph, 1971.
Spruce, Richard. *Notes of a Botanist on the Amazon.* New York: Macmillan, 1962 (reprint).
Steenis, Van. C.G.G.J. *Rheophytes of the World.* The Netherlands and Rockville, Md.: Sijthoff & Noordhoft, 1981.
Wallace, Alfred Russel. *Narrative of Travels on the Amazon and Rio Negro,* Reeve & Co., 1905, and Magnolia, Mass.: Peter Smith Publisher (reprint of 1889 edition).
Walsh, John and Robert Gannon. *Time Is Short and the Water Rises.* London: Nelson, 1967.

Want to do an unusual river trip in South America—or elsewhere? Need companions or information?

Let us tell you how we can help you with your ideas.

'Great Expeditions' is a membership organization for the adventurous traveler and explorer.

We have many useful services, run our own trips, have meetings throughout North America, publish 6 issues of 'Great Expeditions' newsmagazine a year, and more.

Join the adventurous explorers. For details, write: 'Great Expeditions', Box 46499, Station G, Vancouver, B.C., Canada V6R 4G7.

Published annually in November, the encyclopaedic

South American Handbook

including the Caribbean, Mexico and Central America.
Nearly 1,300 pages with 8 pp. colored sectional maps.

"The best guidebook on South America"

Available from your bookstore, or direct from
Trade & Travel Publications, Bath, England.

WINNER OF THE THOMAS COOK TRAVEL BOOK AWARD FOR 1981.

U.S. & Metric Equivalents

Conversion formulae:
5,280 feet = 1 mile = 1.609.344 meters exactly
1 mile = 1.6 km   1/4 mile = 400 m.   1 km = 5/8 mile

Kilometers	Miles	Miles	Kilometers
20	12.5	20	32
30	18.5	30	48
40	25	40	64
50	31	50	80.5
60	37	60	96.5
70	43.5	70	113
80	49.5	80	129
90	56	90	145
100	62	100	161

Temperature conversion between Fahrenheit (°F) and Celsius (°C)
°F = 9/5 (°C) + 32°   or   °C = 5/9 (°F − 32°)

°F	°C	°F	°C
−40	−40	77	25
0	−18	98.6	37
32	0	104	40
68	20	212	100

1" = 22 millimeters
1" = 2.2 centimeters
36" = .9144 meter
39.37" = 1 meter
1 knot = 1 nautical mile per hour (Spanish: *Nudo*)
1 nautical mile (6,076') = 1,852 meters
1 fathom (6') = 1.83 meters (Spanish: *Braza*)

Martin and Tanis in their Avon Redseal inflatable. Coppename River, Surinam.

Index

Acanan (R) 95
Albina (P) 64 78
Amazon (R) 37 94 99
Angel Falls (P) 53 – 60
Annapaike (P) 88
Aonda Canyon (P) 54 56
Arinos (R) 101

Bigisante Beach (P) 70 –74
Bitagron (P) 68
Boa Vista (P) 93
Branco (R) 92
Brinkheuvel Reserve (P) 64
Brownsberg Reserve (P) 65
Brownsweg (P) 65

Canaima (P) 53
Caracarai (P) 95
Caroni (R) 34
Carrao (R) 54 56
Catrimani (P) 95
Churun Canyon (P) 54 60
Cocha Cashu (P) 104 106
Coppename (R) 66
Coppename Monding Reserve (P) 64
Corantijn (R) 81
Cuiabá (P) 100
Cumerjali (R) 79
Cusco (P) 103

Dinquira (R) 108

Eilerts de Haan Reserve (P) 67

Galibi Reserve (P) 64
Guaporé (R) 94 100
Guajará Mirim (P) 100

I de Marajo (P) 92

Juruena (R) 95

Lawa (R) 78 87

Madre De Dios (R) 109
Madre De Dios (Alto) (R) 103
Maldonado (P) 109
Manaus (P) 94
Manu (P) 39
Manu (R) 104 – 106
Marowijne (R) 87 90 103

Negro (R) 93

Pakitsa (P) 103
Panagua (R) 104
Pantiacolla (R) 109
Paradise (P) 67
Paramaribo (P) 63 65 66 78 91
Pinquen (R) 106
Porto Velho (P) 99
Pucacungayo (R) 106

Raleigh Falls (P) 66 69

Santarem (P) 101
Shintuya (P) 102
Sinop (P) 100
Sipaliwini Reserve (P) 63
Stoelmanseiland (P) 78
Surinam (R) 69

Tafelberg Reserve (P) 63
Tapajos (R) 99
Tapanahoni (R) 80
Teboe Top (P) 81
Teles Pires (R) 100

Ucaima (P) 96

Voltzberg Reserve (P) 67 – 69

Wia Wia Reserve (P) 70 72

Xingu (R) 95

R = River   P = Place

Hungry explorer kneads the dough....

...wraps it round the stick for his stick-bread.....

...and bakes it over the glowing...while reflecting upon the efficiency of embers of his camp fire.... common domestic cooking appliances back home in civilization......

A Guide to the Birds of Venezuela
Rodolphe Meyer de Schauensee
William H Phelps, Guy Tudor
Princeton University Press 1978
Princeton New Jersey.

Birds of South America - Schauensee